TO THE MEMORY OF MY UNCLE OLIVER MESSEL

SNOWDON
PERSONAL VIEW

DESIGN BY BARNEY WAN

WEIDENFELD & NICOLSON, LONDON, IN ASSOCIATION WITH CONDÉ NAST

I would like to pay particular tribute and thanks to everyone at *Vogue*, and *The Sunday Times*, who have given me their encouragement, advice, and endless time: especially Beatrix Miller, Alex Kroll, Felicity Clark, Lillie Davies, and Michael Rand (art director of *The Sunday Times* Magazine); to William Green for the interviews on which the text is based, to Mark Boxer for editing it; to Terry Lack for printing my black-and-white photographs superbly for the last ten years; to Terry Boxall, Barbara Parsons, Dorit Christiansen for retouching and Dudley Mountney, Chris Clark for the photostats; to Dorothy Everard for the mammoth task of finding all the negatives and generally making my work possible by assisting me day in, day out, for the last twenty years; to Stephen Kibble for his tireless contribution since the concept of the book, assisting Barney Wan; and of course to Barney himself for his inexhaustible energy, meticulous care, and inscrutable talent for choosing the photographs and designing the book.

SNOWDON

First published in Great Britain by George Weidenfeld and Nicolson Limited
91 Clapham High Street, London SW4 7TA

ISBN 0 297 77715 7

Printed in Great Britain by Westerham Press, Westerham, Kent

CONTENTS

BIOGRAPHY

Tony Armstrong Jones was born on March 7th, 1930, the son of Ronald Armstrong Jones, a successful barrister, and Anne (née Messel). His background was a professional one. His grandfather, Sir Robert Armstrong-Jones, had pioneered early research into mental health. He once cured a man who believed his actions were determined by an eel inside him, by operating on his stomach, then leaving a live eel in a basin by the patient's bed. His great grandfather on his mother's side was Linley Sambourne, for forty years political cartoonist on *Punch*. Sambourne made an early collection of 12,000 photographs, many of them his own, which he used to ensure the accuracy of his drawings. The name Linley came from earlier ancestors, the Linley sisters of Bath, famous beauties, one of whom eloped with the playwright Sheridan. Another ancestor was Alfred Messel, the architect of the Wertheim Department Store in Berlin and a pioneer in the use of metal and glass. The Messel side of the family included the founder of Messels, the City bankers, and Oliver Messel, who dominated English theatre and opera design for thirty years.

Top The photographer, aged three, with his sister Susan in the gardens of his grandparents' home, Nymans, in Sussex, 1933

1943 Left prep school. Headmaster's report read "Armstrong Jones may be good at something, but it's nothing we teach here." Went to Eton. Mostly interested in science and engineering.

1945 Revived Eton Photographic Society. His picture of Upper School after bombing criticized by the Eton *Chronicle*: "This photograph would have been more lively if there had been people in it."

1948 Abandoned plan to go to Massachusetts Institute of Technology. Went to Jesus College, Cambridge. Read Natural Sciences for ten days. Changed to architecture. Bought first large camera, a secondhand Thornton-Pickard ($3\frac{1}{2}'' \times 2\frac{1}{2}''$ single lens reflex). Most early photographs used for architectural work, but did a few portraits.

1950 Coxed Cambridge in the Boat Race. Won by 3 lengths. The only time in the history of the Boat Race that the oars touched. Failed exams. Left Cambridge.

Left Snowdon's grandmother, Mrs Leonard Messel, who as Maud Sambourne at the age of 15 drew the sketch, right, for 'Punch'. She was a regular contributor from age 15 to 18

Ronald Armstrong Jones and son, 1945

Above right Linley Sambourne, 'Punch' political cartoonist; <u>above left</u>, one of his drawings of Venice

Snowdon's mother with her son, William, taken with his 1936 Roleiflex in 1950

Wertheim department store in Berlin designed by Alfred Messel

The best things about Eton were having your own room, privacy and the freedom of choice to pursue almost any subject or activity.

Heath Robinson would, I think, have approved of my room – it was stuffed full of electronic gadgets, flashing lights and wire pulleys. The black-out curtains drew automatically when you opened the door; a system of flashing lights wired to switches under the lino in the passage warned of possible unwanted intruders. There was also a burglar alarm on the food cupboard. I was once beaten for making my fagmaster's toast on an electric toaster I had made, instead of using the traditional toasting fork in front of the coal fire

Although wirelesses and gramophones were not allowed, my housemaster unwittingly gave us permission to use anything we made ourselves. So I made a radiogram (*left*), slightly out of cussedness: he couldn't go back on his word. The privacy I valued so much disappeared overnight – I only had three 78's but that didn't seem to deter the audience.

After I was ill I made more gadgets. One of them was a walking stick which unscrewed in lots of places and contained a crystal set and torch at the top. While watching games, with an aerial up my sleeve and earthed with the walking stick into the ground, I listened to the Home Service through an earphone attached to my top hat.

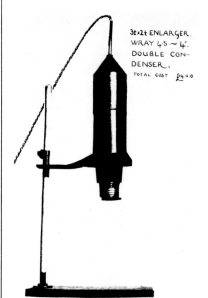

3t×2t ENLARGER.
WRAY 4.5 ~ 4".
DOUBLE CON-
DENSER.
TOTAL COST £4:0:0

I first started printing with a horizontal mahogany enlarger in the dark room of a chemist in Windsor High Street, experimenting at other people's expense with their snaps. Enlargers during the war were expensive, so I made this one myself (*left*) from large tomato soup cans and bits from a scrap heap.

One of my earliest pictures. I glued together with Seccotine a handful of matches to make them look as if they were falling out of the box. It was a flash-gun picture taken without flash.

Telegram from my mother, after I wrote to say I was giving up architecture and taking up photography.

1951 Apprenticeship with Baron. Lived in box-room in Albany. Worked with David Sim doing portraits for *Spotlight* etc. September: first picture published in the *Tatler*.

1952 Converted ironmonger's shop in Pimlico into a studio. First picture spread in *Picture Post*: photographs of flamenco dancers at an Oliver Messel party.

1953 Contributed regularly to the *Tatler* and *Sketch*.

1954 First theatre photocall: Rattigan's *Separate Tables*. Started using miniature camera rather than plate camera for theatre coverage.

Right Montage of Baron, 1951. **Below right** First pay packet from Baron, 1951

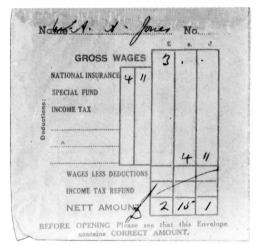

A double exposure of the Archbishop of York – an early example of luck working to my advantage. I was working for Baron and forgot to wind on the film.

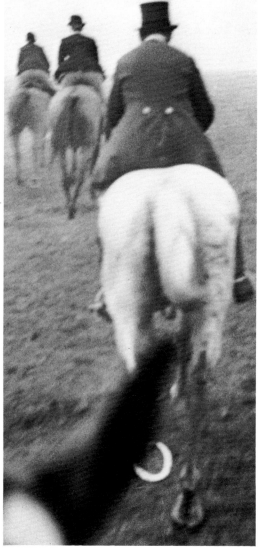

Left Cockle hunting at Blakeney Point, Norfolk; the first photography to appear in the 'Tatler'. An earlier attempt to show work to the 'Tatler' had been foiled by a commissioner who inspected his portfolio saying, "We don't use these kind of pictures, Sonny. Try somewhere else."

Taken from on horseback. I didn't hunt, and could hardly ride, but have great respect for horses, at a distance. I bought riding boots from an old clothes shop in Pimlico. One boot had a brown top, the other was black; but I didn't think it mattered because when mounted, no one would see both legs at the same time. I tied a knot in the reins – very *mal vu* – so I could hold a camera. "We expect to be photographed at the meet," said a young debutante, "but it's very unsporting to actually come out hunting with us." I thought it was extremely sporting.

An old woman in Madeira, taken for the 'Tatler' when covering a cruise in 1951

Left Miss Sally Churchill in head-dress Snowdon made for the Golden Cage Ball, 1953

Front page of the 'Tatler', 1954: "One of this year's debutantes who will be remembered alike for her charm and grace is Miss Mary-Anne Hare..."

An unsatisfied customer, 1953

My favourite caption from the *Tatler*: "The Hon. Patricia Cavendish, sister of Lord Waterpark, enjoying the cool depths of the Mediterranean." I took the picture with a home-made underwater camera off Eden Roc in 1953.

My uncle, Oliver Messel, was a very strong influence on my life and work. When I was six, he let me help him make some masks in his studio for a Cochran revue. Later I went with him on my first visit to Venice, where he taught me to use my eyes.

He was unquestionably the outstanding theatre designer of his day. In 1932 his white on white set for Cochran's *La Belle Hélène* got a standing ovation every night: it had an enormous influence on interior decorators of the Thirties. He developed his own kind of romantic baroque with productions at Covent Garden and his costumes and sets for Glyndebourne, which were what everybody longed for after the austerity of the war. He had a flawless sense of colour; but he will perhaps be best remembered for his own original form of romanticism in *Ring Round the Moon* and *House of Flowers*.

He was a master of illusion and make-believe; often you'd find that he'd personally made a chandelier with sticky paper and fuse-wire, or constructed the dancers' head-dresses out of pipe cleaners. When I was a child I found a bird's nest in his London garden; on inspection I discovered it was made by him and the eggs were china and hand-painted.

He was extremely practical, making all his own models, down to the last detail. He had the respect of everyone in the theatre because he knew which way the fabric was cut and how every prop could be made. He would work all night. He had endless energy, was very strong willed, in fact a perfectionist.

Oliver Messel in his garden in Pelham Place with Cecil Beaton

Left Housemasters watching football
in the fog at Eton, 1953
Below left The Headmaster's letter
Below Family group. Sent to friends as
a Christmas card in 1954

FROM THE HEAD MASTER

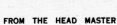

WINDSOR 439

ETON COLLEGE,
WINDSOR,
BERKS.

16th February, 1953.

Dear Mr. Armstrong-Jones,

      I understand that you were responsible for taking
a number of photographs at Eton of boys coming back at the
beginning of this half. As you were with your half brother,
Martin Parsons, whose photograph you took, I take it that the
information I received was correct.

      I should be glad to have an assurance from you that
you will not take photographs again in that way about Eton without
obtaining our permission first. I may say that this permission
would not be granted for photographs of this kind. We realise
that on certain occasions, such as the Fourth of June, the
situation is rather different, but we do not want to have photographs taken generally of boys while at the school in the way
that was done for this number of The Tatler.

                  Yours sincerely,

A. C. R. Armstrong-Jones, Esq.,
Coombe Place,
Offham,
Lewis, Sussex.

1956 First pictures, mainly theatrical, appeared in *Vogue*, American *Vogue, Harper's Bazaar*, and *Daily Express*. First large displays and blow-ups used for front of house, in place of conventional framed 10 × 8 prints.

1957 First exhibition at Kodak House, Kingsway. Asked to take official pictures of the Queen and her family. Began regular contributions to *The Queen* magazine covering Cruft's, Henley Regatta, Chelsea Flower Show etc. In the words of the proprietor, Jocelyn Stevens, became "The eye of *The Queen* magazine". First fashion pictures for *Vogue*.

Top right Cut-out silhouette of Henrietta Nevill, 1763, and (<u>top left</u>) her descendant, Angela Nevill, photographed in 1954

Above left The children of Sir Edward Ford, then assistant Private Secretary to the Queen. These photographs led to the first Royal commission, photographing the Queen's children, Princess Anne and Prince Charles (<u>above right</u>). The globe was a hired prop. The photographs were for the eighth birthday of Prince Charles. The relatively informal pictures were received by the press as "off-beat" and "unconventional studies". "The end of the old stuffy era in princely portraiture," said the 'Express'

There were only going to be twenty minutes available to do the pictures of the Queen and her family; so I got permission to go along before and submit a sketch for approval. I planned a photograph based on eighteenth-century romantic paintings. The Queen and Prince Philip would be leaning over the bridge in the garden of Buckingham Palace watching the children below catching trout. I hired a rod and bought two trout from the fishmonger. The sketch was approved. On the morning of the assignment, Mrs Peabody, who looked after me in Pimlico, came in with breakfast. "I thought you needed a good start to the day today," she said; and I took off the lid to find she had grilled the trout quite beautifully. The released photograph shows the children reading a book instead.

Facing page The Queen and her family in the garden at Buckingham Palace. **Below** The original sketch

Wedgwood souvenir mug designed for the Queen's Jubilee, 1977. The head was a line print from a photostat sent in by a Canadian admirer who wanted to order a good print

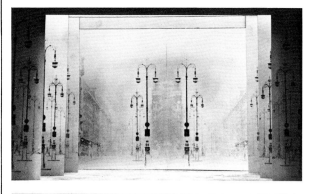

Grainy high-key photographic sets for 'Keep Your Hair On'

From 'Malta' by Sacheverell Sitwell

My ski designs for ladies (*right*) were basically a protest against the English habit of buying ski clothes with a view to next summer's golf. I designed smocks based on French railway porters' uniforms; the knickerbockers were 'borrowed' from my prep school outfit. Every editor from *Vogue* came along to the opening, but they didn't sell at all. I suppose they might have been ahead of their time. Which isn't clever – it's bad timing.

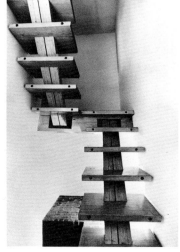

Right Open tread pine and steel staircase for country studio, 1969. **Far right** Early DIY circular staircase made with brass tubes and oak treads. Both took half an hour to assemble

1958 Designed photographic sets for *Keep Your Hair On,* devised by John Cranko; closed after two weeks. Designed collection of ski clothes for women. First visit to New York with Penelope Gilliatt, worked for British and American *Vogue.* Published two books: *Malta* with Sir Sacheverell Sitwell published by Batsford and *London* for Weidenfeld and Nicolson.

1960 Married Princess Margaret. Closed studio in Pimlico.

1961 Began work on Aviary for London Zoo, Regent's Park; opened in 1965. Joined staff of Council of Industrial Design. Signed contract to work exclusively for *The Sunday Times,* mainly for the new colour supplement.

1964 Became member of the Arts Council. Started features for *The Sunday Times* magazine on various social problems: *The Old.* Photographed feature on Nureyev for *Life.*

1965 Published *Private View* with Bryan Robertson and John Russell, a study of the art world in London. Published by Nelson and Time/Life Books. *Some of our Children* on child neglect for *The Sunday Times.*

1966 Issue of *The Sunday Times* magazine devoted to Indian coverage. Written by David Holden. Fourteen-page essay in *Life* on the English theatre; text by Penelope Gilliatt. *Loneliness* feature in *The Sunday Times.*

1967 Essays on vanishing Venice and booming Japan for *The Sunday Times* magazine.

1968 First TV documentary, *Don't Count the Candles,* about old age. Made for CBS with Derek Hart and edited by Jules Laventhol, it won seven awards including two Emmies, and was shown in 22 countries. *Mental Health* feature in *The Sunday Times.* Designed chairmobile which went into production in 1972.

Above **Model for the Regent's Park Aviary.**
Right **Gothic bird-cage, designed in 1959.**
Below **Oriental lakehouse, 1968**

I was commissioned to photograph Venice in black and white for a book for Olivetti; I then persuaded them to do it in colour so that I could photograph it in the soft colours of the winter mist and fog. I wanted to show the life and people of Venice rather than the architecture; it's always worrying putting the camera to your eye and finding a Canaletto in the viewfinder. Olivetti published 25,000 copies to give away. Sadly it was never available on the bookstalls.

1969 In charge of visual aspects of the Investiture of Prince Charles as Prince of Wales at Caernarvon. Commissioned Carl Toms as designer, emphasized simplicity, got rid of awnings and red carpets to open up the ceremonial for television cameras and to let the castle speak for itself.

1970 Started working for British *Vogue* again. TV documentary, *Love of a Kind,* about incongruous British attitudes towards animals; made with Derek Hart, who also worked on the next two documentaries. Feature on *Children under Stress* in *The Sunday Times.*

1971 TV documentary *Born to be Small* about the problems of people of restricted growth.

From 'A View of Venice' for Olivetti

1972 Published *Venice,* a book commissioned for private distribution by Olivetti. Essays on Peru for *The Sunday Times* and the Amish for *McCalls.* Photographic exhibition and book, *Assignments.* The exhibition, having been turned down by the Kensington store, Derry and Toms (now closed), was shown first in Cologne, and subsequently at the Ideal Home Exhibition, Olympia, and in the US, Far East and Australia. Seen by a million and a half people.

1973 TV documentary *Happy being Happy.*

1974 Made two films for the BBC Explorer series, *Mary Kingsley* in Gabon and *Burke and Wills* in Australia. First time directing actors.

1975 *Sunday Times* feature: *Children behind Bars.*

1978 Brazil for *The Sunday Times.*

1979 With Bill Brandt, made a fellow of the Royal Society of Arts, for photography. Royal Photographic Society Hood award for "promoting concern for children, the disabled and the generally underprivileged".

Photographing white Beluga whales, 1968

A still from TV documentary 'Don't Count the Candles'

Filming in Alice Springs, Australia, on the explorers Burke and Wills

The chairmobile (*above*) was really a very simple idea. It's a highly manoeuvrable platform on which you can put *any* chair and replaces the tubular wheelchair that looked like an old piece of plumbing. The idea was that you shouldn't be visually different if you are sitting behind a desk or in a restaurant. The wheelchair manufacturers wouldn't help – all they had done in years was issue a new colour range for their seats. The *Sunday Mirror* sponsored it on a non-profit basis and sold about 5,000 at £100 each.

My first job as a professional photographer was as an assistant to a well-known society photographer known as Baron. My father paid him £100 to take me on for a three-year apprenticeship. I left after six months. Baron's talent lay in taking extremely good ballet pictures; but his bread and butter came from portraits of debutantes and captains of industry. He ran a photographic factory of the highest quality, but this side of his work had little to do with photography as I saw it. He had a staff of thirty helping him churn out five sittings a day at thirty guineas a time. The finished photograph, mounted on cream card, was heavily retouched and colour prints were hand-tinted. The 'clients' would be seated on a reproduction gilt chair in front of a reproduction tapestry. They were lit with a repetitive formula of arranged spotlights, a left-over from Hollywood in the Thirties – one main light to thin the face and give a sharp shadow under the nose, four back lights, two for the hair and two for the hands, and a small spot near the camera called an Inky Dinky to make the eyes sparkle and soften the shadows. Sometimes he'd say "Right, we'll give her the Rembrandt", which meant shifting the main light a little to the side so the shadow moved daringly across her cheek.

Baron was extremely successful. Sitters got exactly what they wanted – a flattering image that went well in a silver frame on the grand piano. He wasn't too keen on my experimenting in a more naturalistic way, and soon I was banished from the studio to work outside the dark-room in the basement feeding prints into a rotary drying machine like an electric mangle. I frequently used it as a trouser press before going to a party. Unfortunately one evening I heard Baron coming downstairs, showing some VIP round the studio. My trousers were halfway round the drum and I was caught in my underpants, vainly trying to retrieve them.

I left the next week and started working on my own in David Sim's basement studio in Shaftesbury Avenue. I thought I knew it all and would straight away achieve a fresh approach to portrait photography. In fact all I was doing was churning out bad copies of Baron portraits at six guineas a time, with none of his expertise. I spent most evenings taking snaps at parties and Saturdays going to weddings.

By tradition there were two distinct types of wedding photographs: those taken outside the church by the press and then the official commissioned group. For the first, the doyen of the press corps would decree: "We'll take it at fifteen." This meant they would stand at the ready with their plate cameras already focused at fifteen feet in preparation for their single shot. For the second, the 'society' photographer would be waiting with his stand camera, black cloth and lights set up to record the bride with her train impeccably arranged, flanked by the groom, best man, bridesmaids and all the family standing to attention in front of the 'Adam' fireplace.

I tried to free myself from this strait-jacket and treat

Above Before a formal wedding photograph, to be taken by 'Pop' Swaebe, the Hon. Mr & Mrs Anthony Cayzer, 1952
Left Pages stand to attention for the press after a wedding at St Peter's, Eaton Square, 1952

The wedding of Rachel Fitz-Gerald and Michael
Severne at Castle Glin, County Limerick,
Ireland, 1952. It was winter, yet some of the
children from the village were barefoot

Previous page Jane Sheffield before her wedding
to Jocelyn Stevens, 1956. There were 950 guests
at the reception. The bridegroom later bought
'The Queen' magazine

weddings like any other reportage assignment, working with a miniature hand-held camera, using available light, photographing the uninvited as well as the invited. I treated it all rather light-heartedly, capturing moments that were not exactly *comme il faut* at the time. The immaculately turned out bride and groom probably didn't want to be reminded that local children outside the church couldn't afford shoes, nor see themselves in an unguarded moment before the final layer of make-up had been carefully applied.

The first photograph I had published in the *Daily Express* was of Leslie Caron and Peter Hall's wedding. In contrast to most of the weddings I went to, it was a small and secret affair in Marylebone registrar office, although she did wear the conventional long white dress. There were only three guests and I doubled as witness and cameraman. After the wedding she dashed to the New Theatre where she was playing the lead in *Gigi* and I to Fleet Street. The night editor at first rejected it as I asked for a credit. "We never give photographers credits," he said, "and anyway it's out of focus." After realizing there were no other photographs available and it was something of a scoop, he recanted, gave me a credit and a fee of thirty pounds – a great deal more than the six-pound page rate I was used to from the glossies.

Peter Hall carries Leslie Caron over the threshhold after their wedding at Marylebone Town Hall, 1956. Miss Caron was starring in 'Gigi', directed by Hall

CAFE DE PARIS

The Café de Paris was a late-night restaurant on the grand scale, with balconies, red plush and sweeping staircases. In the early Fifties it was run by a certain Major Donald Neville-Willing, known to his friends as Donny Nelly Willy. Most of the outstanding American singers of the decade – Eartha Kitt, Pearl Bailey and Marlene Dietrich – appeared there in cabaret. Donny Nelly Willy allowed me to take pictures from the gallery. I had to wear a dinner jacket, but he gave me dinner. One of the many nights I photographed there, my assistant was so transfixed by Miss Dietrich that he kept on re-loading my camera with the same films. They were re-loaded again and again; not surprisingly they all came out blank. Some pictures another night must have worked – Miss Dietrich saw them, and gave me my first important sitting.

Miss Dietrich is a great professional. Our session took place in the afternoon on the empty Café de Paris stage. I wanted clouds of smoke, but there wasn't enough from her cigarette, so I had three people, including the Major, lying under the piano puffing cigar smoke. I developed the pictures that night and took them round to her after her performance around 3 a.m. She didn't look at the large prints; instead she examined all my contacts minutely without a magnifier. "All right, dear boy," she said, "I like the face in this one, but I like the smoke in that one." "But Miss Dietrich, these pictures have got to go to press this morning." "Then you've got four hours. What you do is you put this one in the enlarger, and you shade this part back with your hands. OK? And then you put it in a drawer; then you take the negative with the smoke I like, and print that one, shading the other bit. Now you go and do that . . ." and she was technically absolutely right. I was never sure if she liked it, until I saw years later that she used it on a record sleeve.

Above **Eartha Kitt, 1956**

Left **Tommy Steele, British rock'n'roll star, 1957**
Right **Marlene Dietrich, 1955**

THEATRE

The West End theatre of the early Fifties was a left-over of pre-war days. Ken Tynan described the average theatrical production of the time as 'Loamshire plays'. The sets were chintzy drawing-rooms and the men in the audience wore dinner jackets. The front of the house was meanly decorated with small production stills which were static, unrealistic, dramatically lit and heavily retouched.

Nearly all the photographs were taken by two famous photographers of the old school, Angus McBean and Houston Rodgers. They used plate cameras which meant they had to use a black cloth and see things upside down, something I couldn't get used to. Technically the pictures were pin-sharp and grainless. Before the play opened in London, a whole day was set aside from rehearsals for the photocall. It always seemed to be in Bournemouth.

The basic technique was to re-light the set, re-stage the 'high points' of the play and re-compose them for the plate camera mounted on a tripod. Every member of the cast had to be included, however small their part and irrespective of whether it made a boring photograph. Actors told you which was their 'best side'. Stars in particular wanted to be photographed as themselves rather than in the character of the part, and expected to have their pictures retouched to make them look permanently young. Remarks like "Angus always takes me from here" didn't help.

My first chance came when Peter Glenville, who was directing Terence Rattigan's new play *Separate Tables*, invited me up to Liverpool to take some rehearsal shots. I took nine spotlights and the regulation plate camera and tripod. But I also packed a miniature camera which I used during rehearsals. One of the pictures of Margaret Leighton (right) was published in *Picture Post*, which, with the pre-war German magazines, had pioneered the use of the miniature camera. But most British magazines and newspapers considered them unsuitable because of the grain.

Working at the Café de Paris had convinced me that photographs taken during performance or rehearsal were far more striking; but the light levels and speed of exposure meant that most of the pictures were grainy because I had to 'push' the film. I refused to use flash which makes everyone look as if they come from Madame Tussaud's. Lenses were long enough then, but they weren't as fast as today. I used to make my own variations, re-matching lenses from different makers to my Leica. Like railway gauges, no lens is ever made to fit an alien camera. I also made an aluminium box lined with rubber for the camera, so it made hardly any noise during a performance.

Newspapers gave little theatrical coverage in the Fifties. The *Sketch* and *Tatler* occasionally published my theatre pictures. But one morning a photograph of mine of Alec Guinness in the Feydeau farce *Hotel Paradiso* appeared mysteriously in the *Daily Express*. The picture had been taken for the management and also for the *Sketch*, to be published in two weeks time. I was summoned to their offices to explain myself. I said I knew nothing about it and wasn't believed for a moment. It then transpired that John Barber, the theatre critic of the *Express*, had un-pinned the photograph from outside the theatre, had it copied for publication and returned it the same night.

John Barber's enterprise resulted in my working regularly for the *Daily Express*. Harold Keeble, the features editor, had started 'Photonews' and he began to use my pictures, blurred or not, across a whole page. Directors were pleased. Particularly as they no longer needed tedious photocalls, wasting a whole day.

Leslie Caron in 'Gigi', 1956

Margaret Leighton in Terence Rattigan's 'Separate Tables', 1954

29

**Laurence Olivier as Archie Rice in
John Osborne's 'The Entertainer', directed by
Tony Richardson at the
Royal Court Theatre, 1957**

I didn't work at the Royal Court until Laurence Olivier appeared there in *The Entertainer*, although my studio, converted from an ironmonger's shop, was just around the corner. George Devine, who ran the Royal Court, was the real hero and patron of the decade. He saw the point of the small camera and encouraged me to change the whole way photographs were displayed outside the theatre. For *The Entertainer* I re-designed the façade of the Royal Court, using huge blow-ups of Olivier. Until then photographs were invariably neatly framed rows of 10 × 8 glossies. I saw it as my job to get people off the bus to go and see the play.

Great stars like Olivier and Guinness go out of their way to help you. When I first photographed Olivier he turned to me and asked me what I would like him to do, and suddenly I was in the terrifying position of directing Olivier. The leaders of most professions invariably make you feel at ease and seemingly have endless time at your disposal.

When Olivier played Archie Rice in *The Entertainer*, the real music hall still existed. I used to go with John Betjeman to the Metropole and to Collins' Music Hall, which was beautifully decorated with tiles from about 1860. You had comedians, up-and-comers, a strip show – real variety in the old tradition. If you got bored with one act, there was a long bar at the back, behind a glass partition.

Collins' Music Hall, one of London's last music halls, 1958

**John Osborne, author of
'Look Back in Anger', 1957**

**Brendan Behan, author of
'The Quare Fellow' and 'The Hostage', 1957**

Brendan Behan from The Theatre Royal, Stratford East, and John Osborne from the
Royal Court in Chelsea, made a pincer movement on the dying West End theatre. Behan
was a serious drinker. I took my sister, who is teetotal, to the sitting, spent mostly in a
Dublin pub. It was 10 a.m. Swearing horribly, Behan demanded she had a drink, and
manfully she asked for "a very large gin".

Theatrical photographs were always retouched to flatter the actors. I did my own retouching, not always successfully, particularly with a photograph of Gladys Cooper in *Night of the Ball*. Traditionally pictures taken on a large camera were retouched on the negative; but because I used a miniature camera I had to work on the final print. I spent hours with a razor blade and dye removing lines from Miss Cooper's handsome features, and put the pictures up outside the theatre. Rather pleased, I took a friend round to see them the next day. To my horror the sun had been on the glass, and the dye had turned bright green. It looked as if a spider had stepped in green ink and walked over her face. Later, when I had stopped retouching to flatter, Gwen Ffrangçon-Davies spoilt the continuity of my front-of-house photographs by taking down my picture of her and replacing it with one of her smiling, specially done for her by Angus McBean. It had nothing to do with the play, but she told me, "I don't want to look like I do in the play, I want to look like me!"

Gladys Cooper in 'The Crystal Heart', 1957

Below Katharine Hepburn in 'The Madwoman of Chaillot', 1969
Right Ingrid Bergman in 'Anastasia', for which she won an
Academy Award, 1957

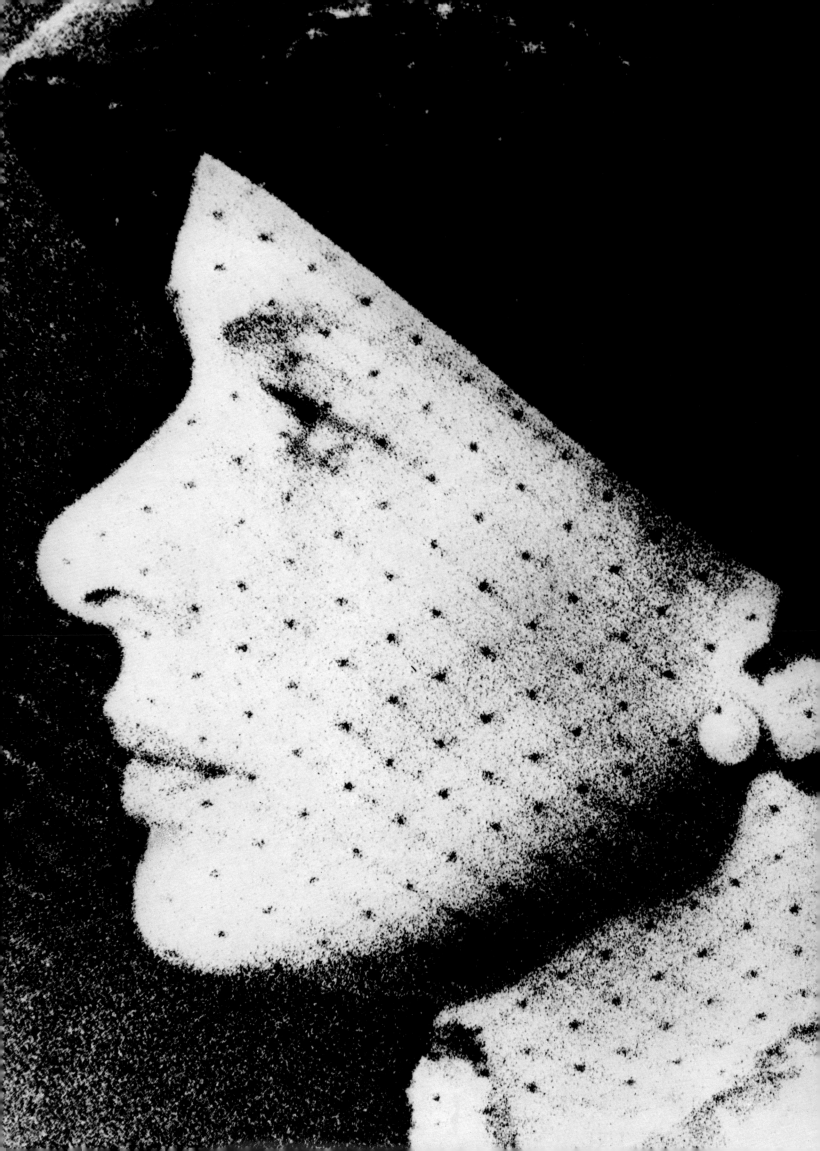

Left John Cranko, choreographer, 1957. He wrote 'The Prince of the Pagodas' to music by Benjamin Britten and created the part of Princess Belle Rose for Svetlana Beriosova, **right**

Johnny Cranko was a great deal more than a choreographer. He broke away from the rarified atmosphere of Covent Garden to direct *Cranks*, a tremendously successful revue which put Anthony Newley and Annie Ross on the map. He did for the dance what John Osborne did for the theatre. By working in the hurly-burly of Shaftesbury Avenue he brought a freshness back to Covent Garden. Eventually he became disillusioned and started a new life in Stuttgart where he built up the ballet from nothing into one of the most accomplished international companies.

He was an enthusiast who was prepared to experiment and give opportunities to unknowns. He did this to me, when he asked me to design the sets for his musical, *Keep Your Hair On*. The set was a combination of huge, grainy semi-abstract blow-ups and extremely complicated mechanical and electrical gadgets. All very self-indulgent and nothing worked on the first night. A gallery first-nighter called Nelly was on top of her form when, after the thirteenth verse of a number called 'Never be a bore', she yelled, very slowly, "Encore". From then on the show fell apart. It was torn to pieces by the critics and closed after fourteen performances.

Left Gloria Higdon, who played in the London run of 'West Side Story', 1958. This picture hung around the offices of 'The Queen' for about a year before they eventually published it, labelled 'Art Director's Picture'
Below Jacqueline Chan, principal dancer in the original London production of 'The King and I', 1955

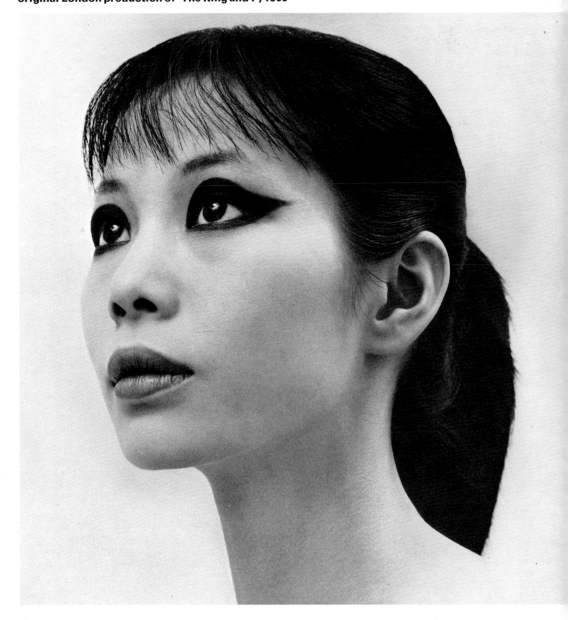

In 1956 Pete[r]
with Paul S[c]
in two of the[
and the Glor[
Reunion. I tr[
looking. In 7[
Scofield's fa[
as if it were t[
light of a wi[
gadget I ma[
aluminium b[
100-watt bul[
three feet wi[
into the bac[
box also wor[
was no wind[
gave me an a[
could move a[
original pict[
surrounded [
looked stilte[
– unlike Car[
cropping ph[
criticism; I a[
than any oth[
sharper than[

Censorship was deplored by the new playwrights. To them the Lord Chamberlain was part villain, part clown in the evolving theatre of the Fifties. Represented usually by some charmer in the Queen's Household, he had the unenviable task of instructing playwrights – whom he would secretly admire – to put indecent language into acceptable public school lingo. Arthur Miller's *A View from the Bridge* met with the Lord Chamberlain's displeasure because of a homosexual kiss. Instead of making alterations, it was decided to put the play on at a theatre club where the Lord Chamberlain had no control. Minor farces of this nature led eventually to the Lord Chamberlain giving up his role as a censor. The first night caused a sensation – mainly because the author brought his new wife, Marilyn Monroe.

My contribution was, for the first time, to take production stills out-of-doors. I took Anthony Quayle and Brian Bedford down to the docks to try for more realism. The set designer didn't like it much.

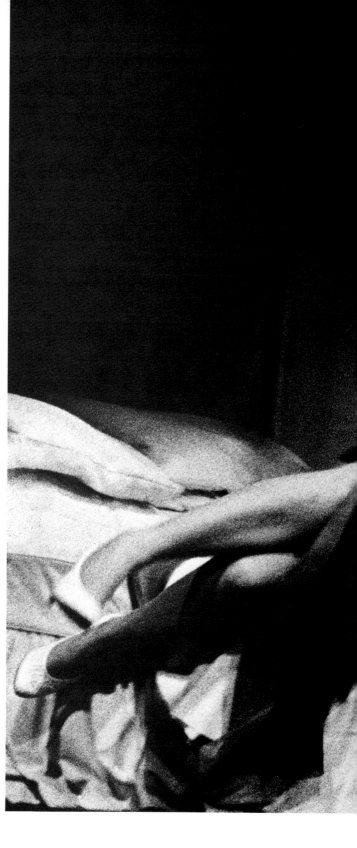

Left Anthony Quayle and Brian Bedford in Arthur Miller's 'A View from the Bridge', directed by Peter Brook, 1956. Taken in the London docks
Above Paul Massie as the drunken Brick and Kim Stanley as his suffering wife Maggie, in Tennessee Williams' 'Cat on a Hot Tin Roof', directed by Peter Hall, 1958. Both plays were banned by the Lord Chamberlain, and were produced for the Watergate Theatre Club

Photographing Alec Guinness in
Feydeau's farce *Hotel Paradiso* was my
first commission for *Vogue*. If you have
taken a weak photograph and have to do
a rescue job, it sometimes works to blow
up a segment of it. I wanted a close-up of
Guinness's head to avoid showing he
wasn't in costume. I had to work from the
stalls, but didn't have a long lens. So I
blew up a section of the negative, using
an 8mm ciné-camera lens in the enlarger
– if I had blown up the whole negative it
would have been twenty-foot square. It
came out grainy and flat. I then put
potassium ferrocyanide on the whites of
the eyes to bleach them, which made it
almost into a caricature.

Alec Guinness as M. Boniface,
the hen-pecked husband in
Feydeau's farce, 'Hotel
Paradiso', translated and
directed by Peter Glenville, 1956

Peggy Ashcroft rehearsing her part of Margaret of Anjou for John Barton's Shakespeare trilogy, 'The Wars of the Roses', at Stratford, 1963

Peggy Ashcroft, taken in what daylight there was, in the rehearsal room at Stratford. I was trying to make my theatre pictures more real, with more feeling of movement, so that my documentary pictures, like the one in Detroit (*page 130*), look almost theatrical in comparison. Again with *Saved* (*overleaf*), I hope it looks as if the pram is being pushed away in life, not on stage. This assignment was for *Life*, around the time Americans became particularly interested in Britain. *Time* had just come out with its 'Swinging London' issue. As far as the theatre was concerned, this was ten years after George Devine and the start of the English stage revolution – probably the most productive period in the English theatre for two hundred years.

**Overleaf 'Saved', by Edward Bond,
directed by William Gaskill, at the Royal Court, 1965**

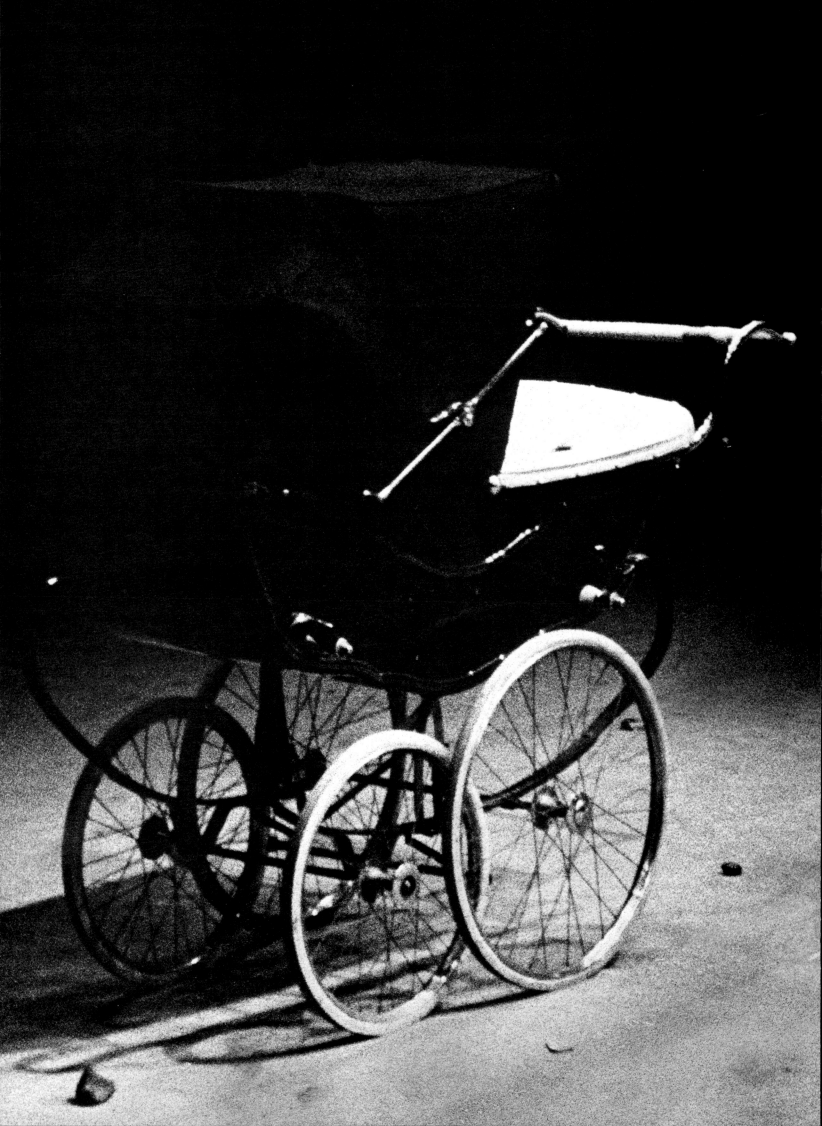

LONDON

I was born in London, but my father was always moving house. "It's too big, it's too big," he declaimed. So we moved. A few months later it would be "It's too small, it's too small," and we'd move again, altogether seventeen times. When I first came to London after Cambridge, I moved into a box-room next to his Albany chambers. He tried to get me a 'proper' job. I had lunch at Messels, a firm founded by my great grandfather; the idea was that I should become a stockbroker, but I couldn't see myself there and left immediately after the pudding. I took a temporary job at £2 a week, working for a flat-letting company, riding round London on a motorbike collecting addresses from postcards outside newsagents' shops; it was at least a good way of getting to know the city. But it was when I began working for *The Queen* magazine in the late Fifties that I first looked at London seriously as a photographer.

I find it almost impossible to work without the pressure of a dead-line or a patron. If I'm given a completely free hand I either turn the job down or quickly become un-interested. Jocelyn Stevens, who owned *The Queen*, was exactly the right kind of patron, enthusing, criticizing, questioning and occasionally ranting and raging. He asked me to photograph tedious annual events like Cruft's or the Chelsea Flower Show. Normally you photo-graphed 'names'. But instead of approaching these events with respect, I treated them with a slight sense of ridi-cule. At Cruft's I photographed the dedicated dog owners and the dogs and forgot the regulation major-generals and their ladies. Rather than photographing the formal opening day of the Flower Show, I preferred to cover the last day when a slow tide of people swamp Belgravia clutching flowers which will die the next day.

I then began to wander round London, with a Leica, a standard lens and lots of film, taking pictures influenced by Cartier-Bresson. I became fascinated by London and its village communities. I had found a room on the river at Rotherhithe and worked from there at weekends and from Pimlico during the week. George Weidenfeld then suggested I do a book on London, which again gave me the incentive I needed.

Nannies in Rotten Row, Hyde Park, London, 1958

Overleaf Oil-magnate Gulbenkian by the Round Pond, Kensington Gardens 1958; a Minox blow-up

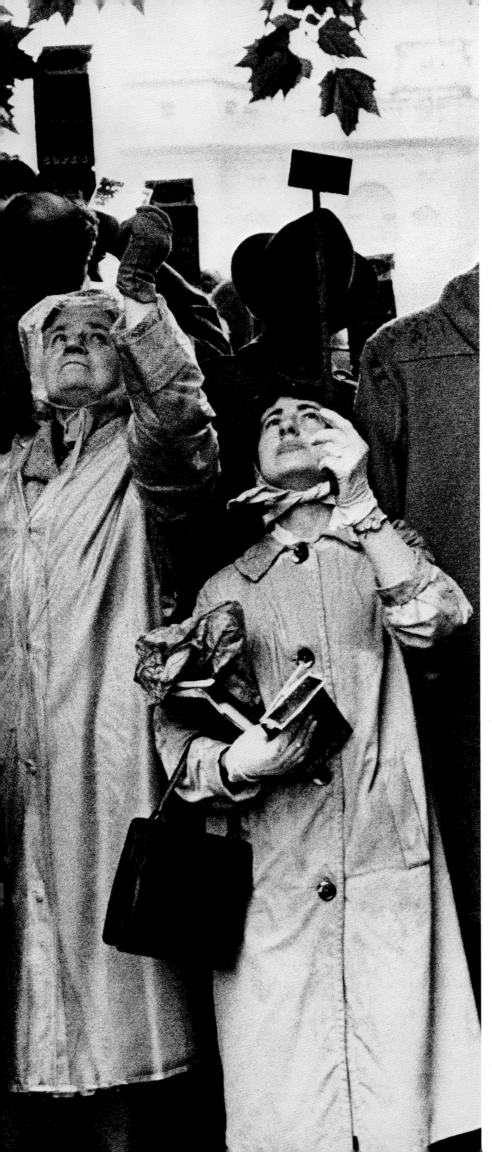

Trooping the Colour, London, 1958

London was a very different city then – almost Dickensian – with vast extravagance and wealth on one hand and great poverty on the other. I tried to illustrate this extremely simply. I didn't want to take photographs for photographers to look at, but rather to make the layman react, to look, to think, to laugh, to cry, but not, I hope, to wince.

The pictures were often out of focus, blurred or badly framed, but I didn't mind about that. You can't say 'Hold it' to real life while you focus. It was exactly what I was trying to capture in the theatre – the mood – to freeze a moment that was typical. All this involved a small camera and available light, which in turn led to grainy pictures, which weren't approved of in those days. For my first exhibition sponsored by Kodak in 1957 I re-designed their main showroom and made it into a maze of huge blow-ups, making it difficult for potential customers to buy film. The day before the exhibition opened I was sent for by the board of directors. They received me sitting round a mahogany table. The chairman said, "Now look here, about this proposed exhibition you're having at Kodak House . . . ." I said, "It's not proposed at all, it starts tomorrow. Leslie Caron is going to open it, and there are two hundred people invited." "Well," he said, "I understand some of these pictures are grainy – very grainy indeed. We at Kodak make high-quality fine-grain film, and we don't wish to see our film promoted in this way." "I shouldn't worry," I told him, "I took it all on Ilford film anyway." They finally demanded I produce a last-minute picture of Annigoni on fine-grain film. They sent two white-coated figures to the sitting with a plate camera, but all their photographs came out blurred: so they used mine, taken with a Leica – still on Ilford film.

**Overleaf right Cruft's Dog Show, at Olympia, London, 1958
Left Acol Ku-Anna, winner of the best toy class, 1959**

**Miss H. M. Loughrey judges a Basenji,
Cruft's, 1958**

Eton-Harrow cricket match, Lord's, 1958

Rehearsals for Prince Charles'
Investiture
Above Lt Commander John
Holdsworth OBE, RN, a gentleman
usher, standing in for Prince Charles,
winter 1969

Overleaf Sunday lunchtime at the
Bridge House Hotel, Canning Town,
1958. Girls from the Windmill Theatre
would work there on their day off, and
men would watch while their wives
cooked lunch

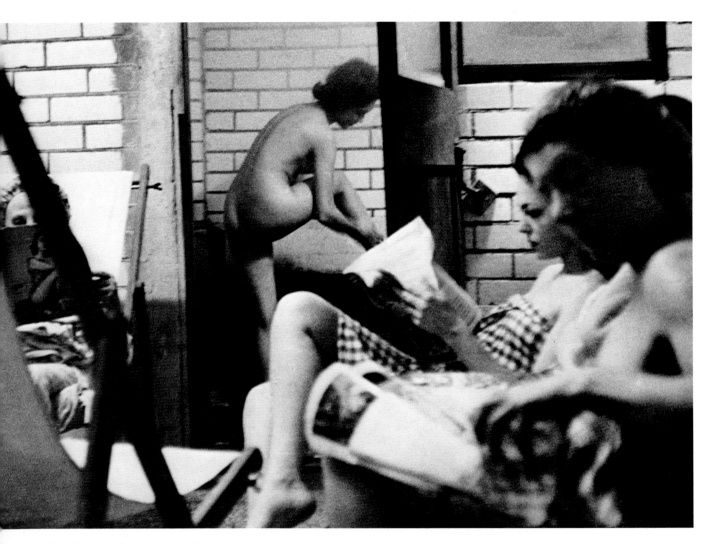

**Ladies' Turkish Baths, Duke of York
Street, London, 1958**

**Lady Lewisham at Monsieur René's
Mayfair hairdressing salon, 1958**

My early fashion photographs were quite simply ... *bad*. Taken for the *Tatler* and *Sketch*, they were hopelessly awkward and stilted. Models used to do their own make-up and hair and even supplied their own accessories. The clothes never fitted, so to make the shape remotely right you stuffed socks down the front of their 'frocks', used bulldog clips at the waist and Scotch tape at the hem. And you retouched like crazy.

For some reason when I started working regularly for *Vogue*, Audrey Withers, the editor, thought she could switch me from the feature pages and make me into a fashion photographer. So I tried. I was at least determined to have fun for myself and hopefully for the reader as well. The models were made to move and react, either by putting them in incongruous situations or by having them perform unlikely and irresponsible feats. I made them run, dance, kiss – anything but stand still. Each sitting became a short story or miniature film strip. To liven up one sitting we invited the cast of *Irma la Douce* to join us. The comedian Ronnie Barker found himself in a lift with one of the fashion editors. "Hello," she said brightly. "I'm Unity." "Well," replied Ronnie Barker, clearly a union member, "I'm Equity."

I liked deceiving the reader's eye. Nylon thread became a favourite device, used to suspend a glass or hold up a house of cards. I would nail the girl's shoes to the floor to defy gravity and suspend her escort with a rope from the ceiling. Air tickets were frequently exchanged for publicity, which explains why nearly every fashion story abroad started with models climbing the stairs into the aeroplane. I just did it without the stairs.

Maybe the *Vogue* readers stopped to look, but I doubt if it helped to sell the clothes one bit. The only thing that could be said is that the photographs didn't imitate those elegant pictures by Irving Penn which I admired so much and which showed the clothes with such style.

I went to New York for the first time on a fashion trip with Penelope Gilliatt who was *Vogue*'s features editor, and of course not remotely interested in fashion. We were amazed by the energy and style of New York. I held the door open for a lady on my first day and she said, "Gee, you must be English." When I asked a taxi driver, "I wonder if you'd be so kind as to take me to 163 East 70th Street?" he said "I'd *what*? What's the address?"

What hit me most was the brashness of the colours; the light seemed harder, the car dumps were like skyscrapers, people walked like a speeded-up movie. I asked Hermione Gingold, who was working in New York at the time, why all that steam came out of the manholes in the street. She said, "I don't know darling. It's either an Indian reservation, or else they're trying to elect a new Pope."

Contact sheet for a 'Vogue' fashion sitting, 1959. The girl's shoe was nailed to the floor, and the man suspended by rope, later retouched out

I stayed on for a bit, working in the New York theatre, and for American *Vogue*, doing beauty shots for one of their formidable editors, Margaret Case. Now you absolutely can't work for American *Vogue* and not have your own telephone, and Miss Case asked me for my number. Two weeks before I had photographed fifty Father Christmases having breakfast together in the Bowery, so I had the number of the Santa Claus at Macy's department store, which I gave to Margaret Case. She would ring it up and bark "Mr Jones, where are you? You're late for an assignment." The answer she'd get was a voice saying "Ho, ho, ho, little girl, now what would *you* like Santa to bring you?" And she'd say, "Mr Jones, would you mind sobering up, we have a *very* important sitting in ten minutes."

I had never been in a skyscraper before so when I had a session with Mrs William Paley, who appeared endlessly in *Vogue* sitting on a sofa, I had her leaning out of one window miles up, and I was leaning out of another. Margaret Case exploded: "I don't understand you, Mr Jones, all this leaning out of windows; you can't treat *personalities* like this. When Cecil takes a photograph he just sits people down." In the end I persuaded Miss Case to provide the smoky background I wanted. I got her first to stand behind Mrs Paley, then to kneel, and eventually to lie under the bed puffing at a cigar. After that we were inseparable and I got a telephone.

FASHION

ACRILAN   FOR AN ACTIVE LIFE!

Advertisement, 1957, shot on the staircase of the Pimlico studio
Below left Two unexpected advertisements to promote 'The Queen' magazine, 1958
Bottom left Advertisement, 1958. The cards were held with glue and nylon thread
Below Fashion shot, Victoria Station, 1959

Pagan Grigg, in 'Vogue' picture at Idlewild Airport, New York, 1958

Fashion sitting with the cast of 'Irma la Douce', 1958

Advertisement: 'Acrilan for an Active Life', 1957

Fashion sitting in New York, 1958

June 'Vogue', 1957.
The glasses were held in
place with nylon thread

'Vogue' summer
fashion picture 1959,
taken in midwinter
at Rotherhithe
on the south bank
of the Thames

Marla Landi at the ski resort of Cervinia, Italy. Advertisements for Sekers, 1958

If I'm taking a portrait of somebody, I want to know every single possible thing about them. I believe very strongly in doing my homework. I like to get hold of details of all their work beforehand. Then I talk about them with the writer of the article, on the way to the sitting. I need to become totally involved. During the time I'm with the sitter, I don't want to talk about anything else. It's vital for me to be able to say "Oh, in 1933 you wrote so and so" and they're surprised you know, but flattered. Everyone likes talking about their work.

I sometimes leave them alone and just watch. I need someone else to be there, to talk, to act as a sounding board. I wander round and see what happens, waiting to catch something. Then in the end it has to be played to me. It's important at this point that there should be no distraction. When I get a new assistant, I always take him aside and ask him not to catch an eyeline. Otherwise I find that at the crucial moment the sitter, feeling trapped and wanting to escape the lens, will evade me by catching the assistant's eye and talking to him. Similarly I learned many years ago, when photographing children in Baron's studio, that the cardinal rule was simple: you had to lock out the mothers and direct children like actors. I dislike all distractions. Some photographers like to work with a great sense of activity around them and with a gramophone at full blast. When I am working I need complete silence.

As you get older you dread running out of ideas and you hope you can rely on experience instead, which is not the same thing at all. You fear you are going to repeat a technique you've used before, which isn't helped by wanting to make pictures more simple and less gimmicky.

For a portrait it is essential to get down to some central core. I look for expressions that are typical; something that is uncharacteristic is pointless. Being photographed is embarrassing for most people and it is important to get beyond their mask. If they are well known you are likely to be confronted with a pose you have seen before. When Cartier-Bresson photographed Oliver Messel he wandered round, watching Oliver at work. This rather unsettled Oliver, who, like most of his generation, was used to something more formal. He would stand in a certain way, with a set expression, and wasn't used to being caught off guard.

You have to strip people of all their poses and disguises. Certain muscles tighten up in the face when you are self-conscious or nervous. I sometimes try to break this down by taking an enormously long time – not taking any pictures at all for ages, or having long, boring gaps between each exposure. When I was photographing Peter Ustinov (page 96) he came into the studio full of imitations, quips, anecdotes – but by waiting around I eventually slowed him down. I did it with complete silences for a very long time, sometimes not taking a picture for ten minutes. He half joked his way out of it. But slowly he became rather thoughtful, almost wistful in fact, and I think I got a truer version of the real Ustinov as a result.

Similarly with Perelman (page 97), when he first arrived at the studio he talked about dogs most of the time in an animated manner. I later photographed him in the turret room at the top of my house. It's only about six feet wide; but he comes out as rather an isolated figure – most creative people seem to me to be rather lonely. He had his hat with him – I like accessories if they are not forced.

The eyes are the most revealing clue to the human face; and eyelashes are easy to focus on. I often need to include hands in a portrait; three 'objects' – the face and two hands for example – can be more powerful than two. Two faces are the hardest to compose; photographs shouldn't be too balanced. If you are taking a group it's always better to have uneven numbers.

I use daylight wherever possible, often with bounced light – that is, light reflected by anything from a handkerchief held next to the sitter's face, to a large reflector board. This high key technique was largely evolved in the Fifties by the fashion photographer John French, who had a strong influence on many other photographers like Bailey, Donovan and Duffy, who all trained with him.

I don't like to have too much background now; I never use sky in my photographs – it's a waste of space. Working out-of-doors I often use the background rather like a roll of studio paper. Indoors, particularly with writers, I avoid books as background; they are as flat and visually as boring as bricks. I don't like flat surfaces. A completely calm lake is ugly. You need a ripple to focus on. I am always suspicious if photographs are too beautiful. A camera is only a means of catching a moment of time and a photographer should try to record this brief moment and not make his picture too contrived. I think the most insulting thing you can say about a photograph is that it looks like a painting.

Unfortunately, one tends to lead a butterfly life – you're doing one, perhaps two assignments a day. Over the years you find that you have photographed a great number of people, but you haven't really got to know them well. One of the sadnesses about being a photographer is that you meet so many people you long to see more of, but seldom see again.

Somerset Maugham, aged 84, in 1958

Many people try to imitate John Betjeman, but nobody does it better than he does himself. He must have been a Grand Old Man at the age of eighteen. I've photographed him many times – in Victorian buildings, railway stations, East End graveyards, and pubs with frosted glass. For his latest sitting I decided to put a preservation order on the ancient cardigan he was wearing. When the print arrived at *Vogue* they rang to say did I realize I had overlooked his cardigan gaping open; they would, of course, retouch it.

John Betjeman, Poet Laureate, at Broad Street Station, London, 1972

At home, 1974

When I arrived at Tolkien's house I found it curiously characterless. Before I met him, I had spent hours near his home looking for places that might reflect *The Lord of the Rings*, but had found nothing. When we went for a walk before lunch we came upon this bit of wood about 500 yards from his house. It's one of the few occasions when I've used a wide-angle lens for people, as I don't like the way it distorts. But in this case it helps; the wood becomes flattened out and makes him become part of his surroundings in the mood of his work.

J. R. R. Tolkien, aged 80, 1972

Two philosophers:
Left Sir Alfred J. Ayer, Professor of Logic at Oxford University, in 1975
Right Bertrand Russell, aged 94, in 1967

T. S. Eliot, aged 70, in Edinburgh, 1958

Graham Greene, London, 1966

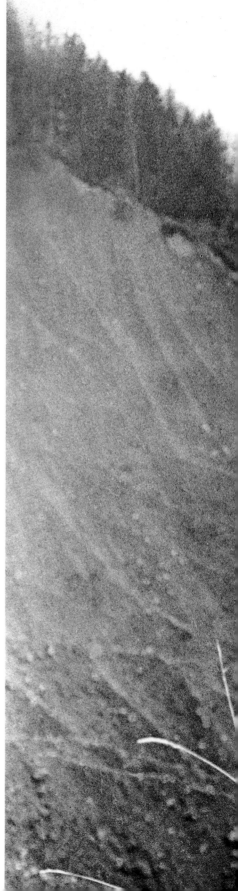

Inexplicable luck plays a large part in taking portraits – not always usable luck, but odd coincidences you can't explain. I was always fascinated by the tricks Nabokov played with words, letters, and punctuation in his books. And strangely, when I took him on to the roof of his hotel in Montreux to take some head shots with a clear background, he noticed one letter of the neon sign naming the hotel had dropped off; seen from the reverse side it spelt 'my own' in Russian. Later I photographed him cocooned in a shawl on the mountain behind Montreux where, in the summer, he hunted butterflies.

Vladimir Nabokov, 1973

Georges Simenon, creator of 'Maigret', 1978

J. B. Priestley, aged 75, in 1969

George Melly, writer, critic, wit, jazz and blues singer, 1973

Ian McEwan, author of 'The Cement Garden', 1978

John Updike, author of 'Couples', 1979

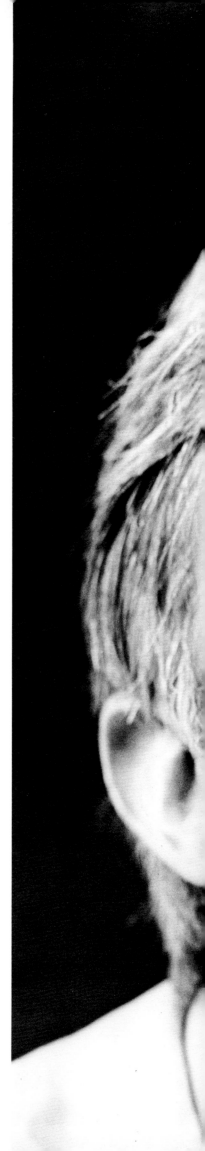

David Storey, author of 'This Sporting Life', 1971

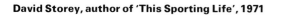

Germaine Greer agreed to be photographed for *Vogue*, which I thought untypical. So I photographed her in a rather feminine way. Earlier, in search of the right location, we went for a walk in the Portobello Road; she was rather disconcerted when a tramp came up and asked if he could kiss her.

Gloria Steinem, journalist, 1971

Lady Antonia Fraser, author of 'Mary Queen of Scots', 1972

Germaine Greer,
author of 'The Female Eunuch', 1971

Three authors:
Left Kingsley Amis with his wife,
Elizabeth Jane Howard, 1974
Right His son Martin Amis, 1978

Tim Rice, lyricist of 'Jesus Christ Superstar' and 'Evita', 1976

I first met Noël Coward at a pub in Battersea. He was playing the piano at The Cricketers' Arms on New Year's Eve and singing 'London Pride' – he was a great Londoner. I always enjoyed listening to him talk. He would unfailingly bring a room alive simply by walking into it. He told me he never knew what it was like to be shy. He was a great commentator, with humour, of the time and the world he lived in. He was sometimes wicked, but never nastily funny. He had the great talent of making other people feel funny too. Within his own drawing-room society, he had, in his early plays like *The Vortex*, been just as much an angry young man as John Osborne.

Peter Cook, actor, satirist and owner of 'Private Eye', 1968

Overleaf left Peter Ustinov, 1979. Right S. J. Perelman, who wrote film scripts for the Marx Brothers, 1978

ART WORLD

In the late Fifties I took occasional breaks from photography. I always find change helps me; afterwards it's refreshing to get back to stills. I enjoyed making and designing things, trying my hand at anything from constructing my own underwater camera to building a Gothic aviary. I designed a collection of ski clothes, though few people bought them. The sales-girls directed everyone's attention to sensible Norwegian sweaters. I started a short film with Wayland Young about an orphan boy on a bomb site, but we ran out of money. In 1959 I applied for a job on Huw Wheldon's television arts programme, *Monitor*, where Ken Russell was already working, but I was turned down.

In the early Sixties I took a job with the Design Council and also started work on the aviary for the London Zoo. I had a wonderful brief – just to make the biggest possible enclosed space. I wanted it to look exciting as a structure from the outside; but from inside I wanted it to be invisible so you concentrate on the birds. As you walk through it over the suspension bridge you can look up, sideways and down at the birds, which works quite well for photographers. It wasn't appreciated at the press show because it needed to be overgrown, and that takes time. Many of the trees that were specially planted inside were killed by bird droppings, while some of the wooden stakes that were hammered in to hold them up flourished, and are now among the biggest trees there.

I've never specialized or planned anything very much at all. Things turn up – different kinds of photographic assignments, a book, an exhibition, a television documentary. I only 'plan' by saying yes or no, depending on how the idea strikes me at the time. In 1962 I was invited to join the *Sunday Times*, mainly working for their new colour magazine. Rival newspapers were jealous of it and hoped the magazine would fail. They claimed it was simply an advertising gimmick of Lord Thomson's devising. (The sternest critics started their own magazine three years later.) The *Sunday Times* magazine had a nerve-racking start and it was some time before it began to be editorially effective.

Taking up photography after a break of two years wasn't a problem for me; I hadn't stopped using a camera. But a reportage photographer needs total anonymity and must blend into the background like a chameleon. This ability is totally lost if your face becomes known through television and the press. Cartier-Bresson seldom allows himself to be photographed, and on one occasion when he appeared on television he insisted on being filmed from the back in silhouette. It's not that I'm instantly recognizable, but particularly at seaside resorts, where people are sitting around using their eyes, I'm often accosted if I have a camera in my hands. They say: "Am I right?" or "I've got a bet with my daughter you aren't." Sometimes I get away with it by saying, "People have often said that," or "No, he's far smaller." If I don't have a camera I'm seldom recognized. It's like meeting your dentist in Alice Springs – you might not know where you had seen him before, however bad your teeth were. But if you saw him walking down Wimpole Street carrying a drill, you would.

One of my initial photographic stories for the *Sunday Times* was the first big piece published on David Hockney. This developed into a series for the magazine called 'Painting Now'. It worked well for me because the artists were usually as engrossed in their work as I was, and their studios were quiet and controlled.

Again it was luck that the timing was right. There was probably more going on in the art world in London then than in any other city. For a few years London became a more important art centre than Paris, and competed successfully with New York. The more features we did for the magazine, the more we were asked to do, until the point came when the two critics I was working with, David Sylvester and John Russell, suggested we did a book.

I knew a little bit about modern art and the co-authors of *Private View*, John Russell and Bryan Robertson, then head of the Whitechapel Gallery, taught me a great deal more. So when I started photographing artists it was all relatively fresh to me. I tried to echo the mood of their work in my photographs. I would happily alter the colour of my transparencies afterwards to match the colour of the paintings to get a tighter link. I don't mind this kind of cheating, so long as it's effective.

I only once showed a painter painting. I found the sculptors easier; there was more activity in their studios and their work is three-dimensional. Possibly I was involved more because I enjoy constructing things myself. The book is probably more interesting now than it was when it first came out. It's not a collection of wonderful photographs, it's a record. Perhaps significantly, the book sold better in America than in England. One thing had changed noticeably since the Fifties. The book was expertly designed by Germano Facetti. When I did my first

Francis Bacon, 1963

book with Sacheverell Sitwell on Malta ten years before, I remember ringing up Batsford and asking them who was going to lay out the pictures. They didn't know what I meant at first; but when I explained, they said, "Don't worry, just send us the illustrations and we'll fit them in. We put in sheets of brown paper marked 'photograph' where there's a gap."

The art world has its pretentious and ridiculous side. After the book was finished I was sent out to Germany with Francis Wyndham to do a piece for the *Sunday Times* on the art collectors of the Ruhr. On our first day we were taken in hand by a solemn gallery owner who wore a huge ring, which he proceeded to show to us. "This", he told us, "looks like a solid gold ring, but no, it is not. It has a diamond hidden inside. This is Art." He was very young and earnest. He told us all about another

artist he had on his books who had totally encased a brand new Volkswagen in a square block of concrete.

Later we were shown round the house of a woman collector in Wuppertal. She had bought things by 'unknowns' she had 'discovered', like a wet dishcloth hanging on a nail, and a sausage sheathed in plaster, which had a tendency to drip in damp weather. She had a pile of dirt in one corner which, she told us, she had paid a great deal of money for. It was a big problem for her to maintain this work of art, because visiting dogs were so fond of it. By this time Francis and I were determined not to be had. I was trying hard to be appreciative, so when I found a glass bottle, beautifully back-lit in a window and filled with little paper-covered objects, I said, "This is marvellous." She turned and said, "Oh, are you hungry? Do please take one." It was just a jar of sweets.

Overleaf Helen Lessore in her Beaux Arts Gallery, 1965

Henry Moore, 1964

David Sylvester, art critic, hanging
'Portrait of Mme Castaing'
for the Soutine exhibition at
the Tate Gallery, 1963

Sir John Rothenstein, director of the
Tate Gallery, in its storage
department, just before his
retirement, 1964

105

Ivon Hitchens, 1965

Salvador Dali, 1959

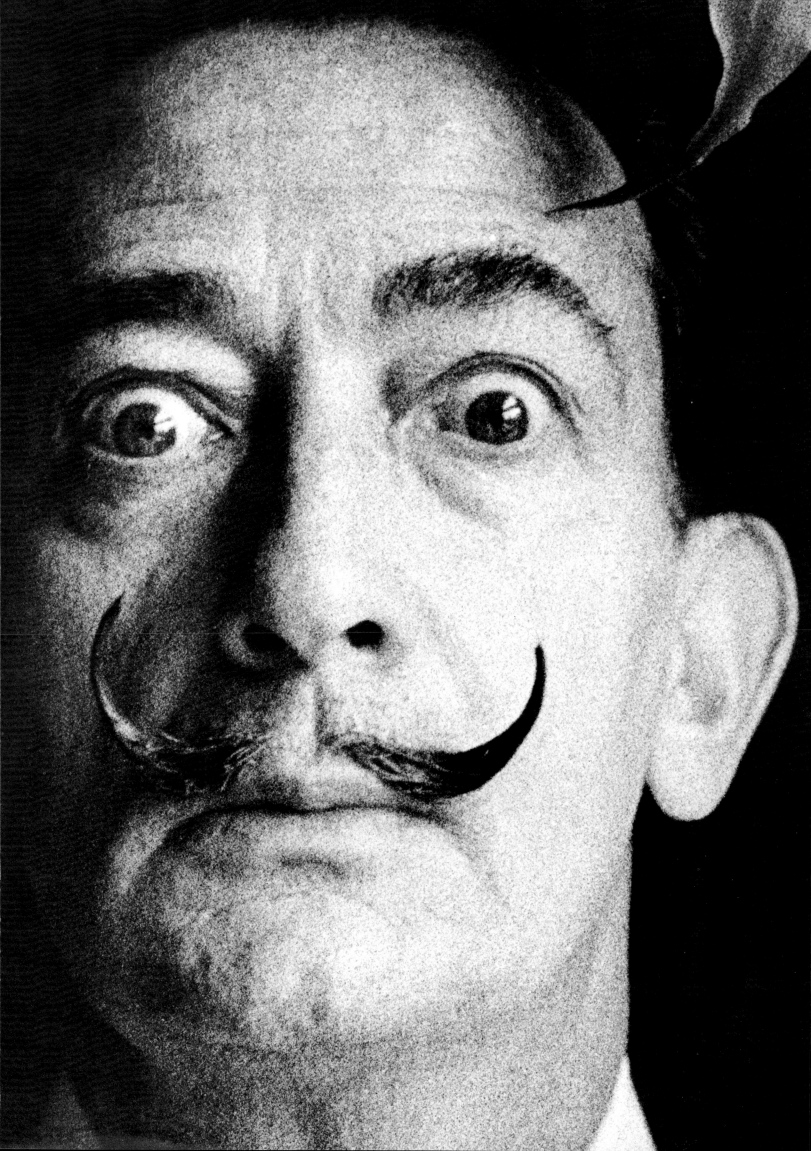

Max Ernst at Huismes, France, remodelling a cement sculpture he had made some fifteen years previously, 1963

Peggy Guggenheim, collector and patron of the arts, in her Palazzo Venier de Leone, Venice, which is also an art gallery, 1976. She was once married to Max Ernst

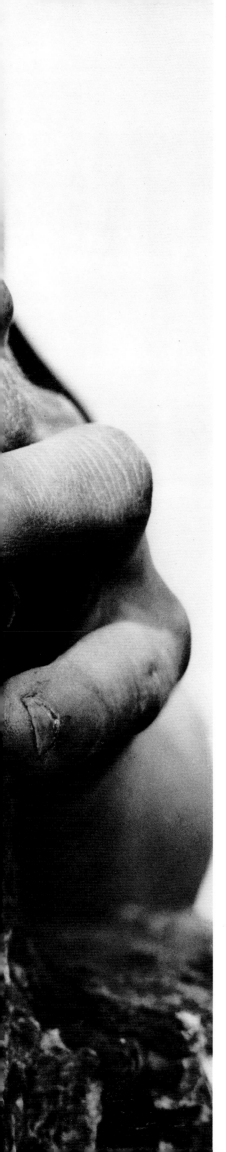

Left and below Reg Butler, 1964 and 1973

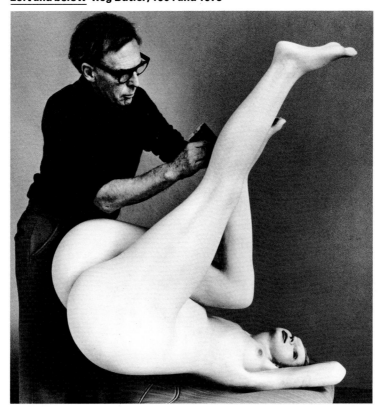

Below Dr Peter Ludwig, chocolate manufacturer and art collector, with Allen Jones' group 'Hatstand, Table and Chair', in the Neue Galerie, Aachen, 1970

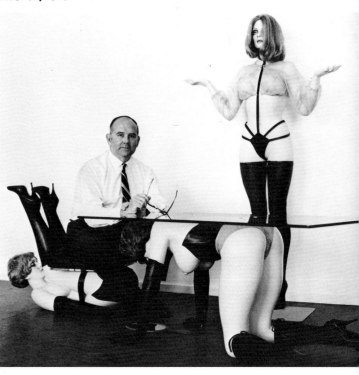

Overleaf Alexander Calder with his wife Louisa at their home in Saché, France, 1967

Willem de Kooning, 1974

Overleaf David Hockney and a pinboard, in his London studio, 1978

Josef Albers, 1970

Ralph Steadman, 1969

David Levine, 1969

The pen of the caricaturist has a particular power to accentuate features, to distort posture, to implant ideas which would be unacceptable in words. Like photographers their exaggeration is legitimate, so long as the technique and style don't overpower the victim. My grandfather was a cartoonist on *Punch* for forty years; and I sometimes like to think I'm a cartoonist who can't put pen to paper, so I have to take photographs instead.

When I photographed Levine, Steadman and Lancaster I asked them to add anything, in their own way. Steadman was the most violent – burning the negative to unrecognizable destruction with a cigarette. David Levine saw himself as Rembrandt and Osbert Lancaster supplied a drawing of Lady Godiva, for no known reason.

Sir Osbert Lancaster, 1958

ON LOCATION

Each time I'm asked to go on an assignment for a magazine, whether it's Peru, India or Africa, I'm filled with dread: the dread of not getting any pictures, the dread of equipment breaking down, the dread of something going wrong in the lab when I get home. All of which is made worse by not being able to see results as you go along.

Luck, and bad luck, play such a huge part in photography. You are so dependent on machinery; a darkroom door can be opened, rolls of film get lost in transit. All of which is compounded when you're abroad. Even the grandest magazines are unlikely to ask for a re-take if it means a return ticket to Brazil. Then, for economic reasons, there's always a lack of time. You are told: "We'd like you to photograph India – three weeks should be enough." How can you bring back anything but a superficial 'take'?

Before setting off, the writer and I work out a rough schedule, do as much homework as possible and then take off with a completely open mind. When I get there I like to stay in boring, anonymous hotels. The first couple of days are the worst, making contacts and getting up at dawn and just wandering. Sidney Nolan once said that the reason Turner was a unique painter was that he just got up earlier than anyone else.

I buy all the local postcards, however awful, to make sure I know all the local attractions. I send them afterwards to my children. Rather than saying "Having a wonderful time" I make them into a quiz: "How does this bridge work?" or "I'm about 180 miles from Detroit and 165 miles from Paris; where am I?" In fact I was photographing the Rodeo (page 217) at a small place called Mary Bell named after the two daughters of a nineteenth-century stationmaster. It took them some time to find out there are two Detroits.

In the evenings the writer and I have endless discussions with local journalists, entrepreneurs and hall porters, trying carefully not to get involved in publicity schemes or falling for "It's never been photographed before" by the local tourist board. In Peru, Norman Lewis and I went miles and miles up a tributary of the Amazon, staying the night in a grass hut, having been told we might just possibly find some Indians who still used blow-pipes and war paint. We got up at dawn, lugging the camera cases through the jungle, then by dug-out canoe across the most beautiful lake, carpeted with water lilies – in the far distance there was smoke rising from the forest. We got very excited; all my cameras were loaded and at the ready. We found the Indians, complete with war paint and blow-pipes. They were being photographed by a group of fifty German dentists with their ladies in khaki shorts and gumboots. Rather than jaguars and monkeys, their blow-pipes were being fired at five-dollar bills; and their war paint had been carefully applied by a make-up artist from the tourist board.

Well-meaning Englishmen abroad can be another time-wasting hazard. Several of the pictures here were commissioned by a solid English company with interests in the Far East. I would fly in with only three days available to reflect their empire's image, to be met by a young public school executive. They always seemed to be called Henry and would shout directions in crude Chinese to the company chauffeur who spoke fluent English. Henry would insist on lengthy discussions and luncheons that robbed me of essential daylight, and in the evening would try to arrange cocktail parties to meet the managing director, "a jolly nice ex-Brit just returned from leave in the UK". He in turn would insist on my going racing in the afternoon to meet the chairman: "It's quite informal. As it's Saturday you can wear brown shoes."

Unloading grain, Bangkok, Thailand, 1976

Pages 122–7 Football, Lagos, Nigeria, 1977 Picnic, Cusco, Peru, 1972 Dominoes, Luxor, Egypt, 1976

**Left and below Members of the Amish sect,
a religious farming community in Pennsylvania**

Some photography is just wandering and looking. I was in Detroit when I photographed this man being arrested. The police didn't like it very much and I too was arrested. I was asked for my papers, but naturally I had left my passport at the hotel and only had my NUJ card. They said it was out of order. I was shoved into open cells with bars. There seemed to be more ladies than gentlemen under arrest. I then produced the visiting card of a policeman I had met a few days earlier at the funeral of a colleague who had been shot. At first this didn't do any good as I was accused of stealing it. Then suddenly everything changed. The sergeant asked me to do a favour and be photographed with him for his daughter. I was about to leave when I was told to wait. I was taken upstairs where the Commissioner of Police sent for the official police photographer to take a photograph of us together for *his* family.

Getting arrested is an occupational hazard of all photo journalists. It happened to me three times in India. Twice for taking pictures of bridges, which was banned by the British before the 1914 war. Ironically you could get postcards of the bridges in question in the local hotels. Another time I was taking a photograph of yellow paddy fields from an aeroplane. I was asked up to the cockpit – I thought they were helping me to get a better view. The captain took my film and cameras and I was arrested on arrival at Bombay, accused of taking pictures of the fleet at Cochin. In the end I took the film out of the camera and gave it to the sergeant. To my amazement he unrolled and exposed it. Holding it up to the light he said "They don't seem to have come out very well." I was eventually rescued by a Chief of Police who introduced himself by saying "I was up at Trinity when you coxed the boat, old chap." He insisted on my having a police escort who rushed out in front of us in the villages, shouting "Come along now, smile for the camera." That day was wasted.

Detroit, 1974

1.R.RICE
2.B.RICE
2.R.RICE
JOLA
CHILLIES
JAGGARY
HUSK

121-00
86-00
37-50

152
26
95
52

RICE
RAGI
JOLA
Broke

London, 1970

PROPRIETORS

Lord Beaverbrook was famous for his staccato utterances, and when I was summoned to Cherkley I was given about three minutes of his time. The picture was published in *The Queen*. Beaverbrook was intrigued by the reputation of the owner, Jocelyn Stevens. "I hear he bites the carpet," he said approvingly. I never knew what he thought of the photograph until I heard it had been made into table mats for the dinner given by Roy Thomson for his eighty-fifth birthday.

Lord Thomson was a complete contrast. He never interfered in the editorial policy of his papers. I designed his office for him. One of the paintings we bought for it, a Sidney Nolan, troubled him. "Am I right to tell visitors it's an atomic explosion?" "No, Roy, it's an elephant."

The photograph was taken in the studio I designed on the roof of the *Sunday Times* – a huge greenhouse with a module of black blinds so that one could have controllable daylight from any direction. Most photographers who hired it pointlessly blacked it out and used flash. One day I came back from an assignment abroad to find it had been converted into the air-conditioning plant.

Lord Beaverbrook, 1959　　　　　**Lord Thomson, 1965**

DOCUMENTARY

In the mid-Sixties I began taking photographs which were very different in subject matter from anything I had taken before. In 1965 I worked on a story on the problems of the old for the *Sunday Times* magazine. Subsequently I did features for them on disabled people, children under stress, spina bifida children and the mentally handicapped. The magazine didn't have to sell on the bookstalls so I could take pictures that were serious, and, if necessary, unprepossessing. My job was simply to make people stop and read the text.

The first story took a great deal of time to get into. Luckily I no longer had a studio or large staff, which usually means photographers have to work quickly to pay their bills or take on assignments they don't want to do. I was able to explore, acclimatize myself and get to know the subject. After some trips I came away without a single roll of film exposed.

I don't want to over-emphasize the misfortunes of people, but on the other hand I don't want to turn a blind eye to them if they happen to exist. I found some of these stories painful and shocking. Many of the conditions I was seeing had not been photographed, or at least published before. There were high walls round many of the institutions I visited which were there as much for the people outside as for those inside. We think of ourselves as a sophisticated society where these kinds of conditions only exist in the third world – which simply is not true.

I was aware of being a visitor. But I was determined not to be a voyeur. Photographically I tried to be as straightforward as possible – no colour, no wide-angle lens shots, no distortion. I wasn't taking fine photographs but wanted to make a simple record of what I saw and experienced. I hoped to break down barriers, but not to shock: I thought if these things were recorded for a better understanding of the situation, then perhaps people would

think more deeply about it, what it meant to the people involved, and what might be done.

Many memories remain: children on remand are surrounded by barbed wire and wardens in uniform; they are treated like convicts before they are convicted. Also the most caring nurses in hospitals and institutions seemed to be West Indian. Perhaps it's because they come from a rural background. If they come from a small village they haven't had to go through all that middle-class politeness and tact. Their response is very direct. Or it may be that their community life is altogether more tolerant.

I have always felt uneasy about intrusion. There is a hair line between reportage and exploitation. This isn't true of war photographers like Robert Capa and Don McCullin whose work I admire enormously. Firstly they cannot stop the wars they witness; and secondly, if their pictures are taken with compassion, publication may do something to make people realize the full horror and stupidity of war.

When you are behind a camera, you are one plane apart. The ground glass viewfinder distances you from reality, in the same way as a disaster on the small television screen is much less alarming than it would be in life. When I was photographing some children in Liverpool living in appalling conditions, I found myself thinking of how to get it all in – the damp coming through the walls, the dirt, the worn face of the mother; and when I looked up from the viewfinder, I saw that the writer of the story, Priscilla Chapman, had been more directly affected; she was suppressing tears.

Such a photograph can have an impact that has nothing to do with photography. The greatest compliment I have ever been paid was by a mother after seeing my exhibition, which included photographs on the next twenty-five pages. She said "Thank you", and when asked why, she said "Now I kiss my son goodnight".

Here, and on the following six pages, part of two features from 'The Sunday Times', 'Some of our Children', 1965, and 'Children under Stress', 1970

THE SUNDAY TIMES *magazine*

MAY 10, 1970

Patricia Byrne has lived
all her life in this
condemned Liverpool street.
A report on children
under stress begins on page 10.
Photographs: Snowdon

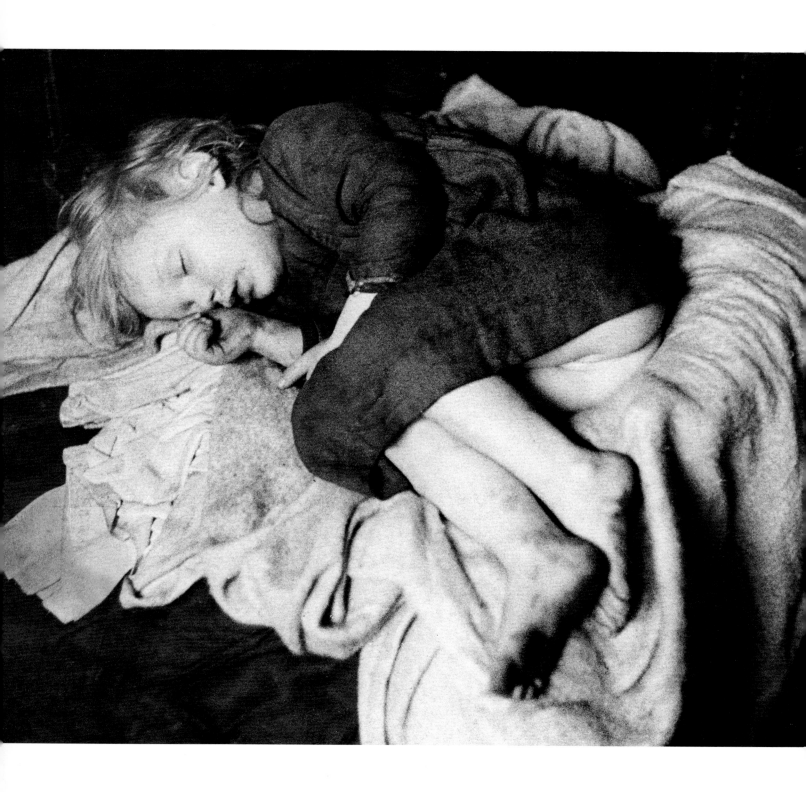

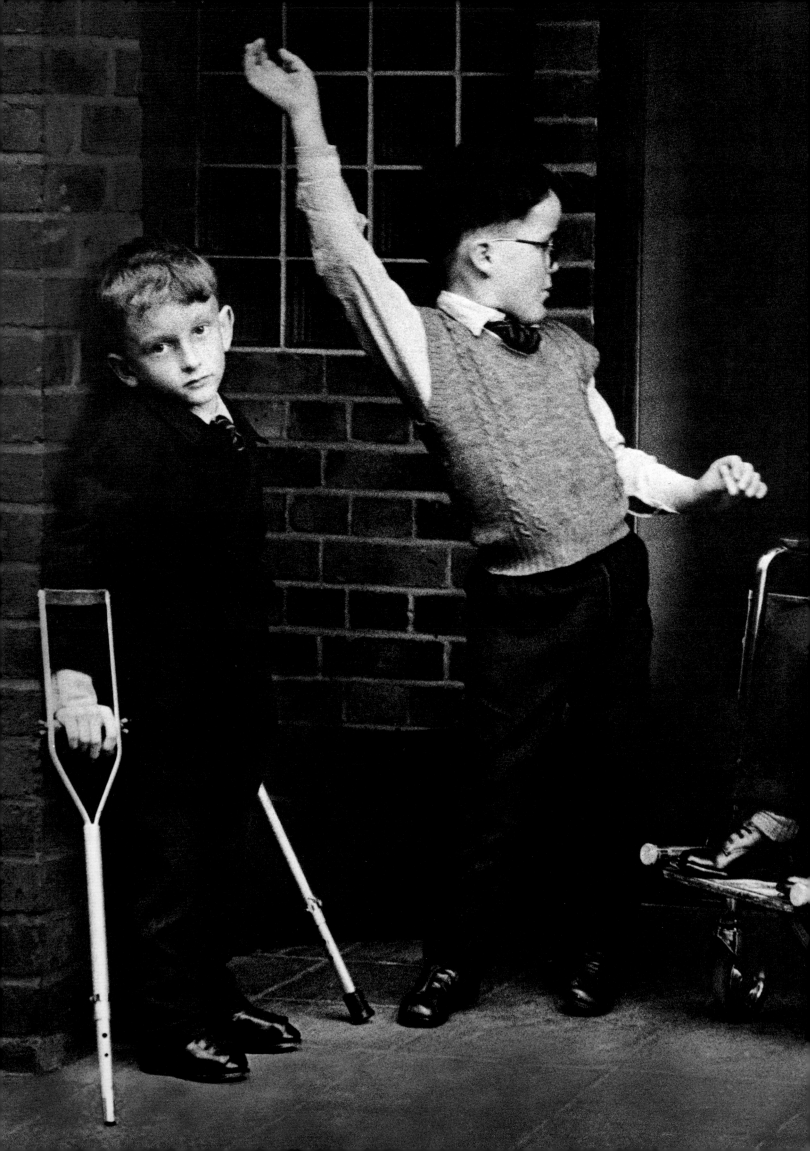

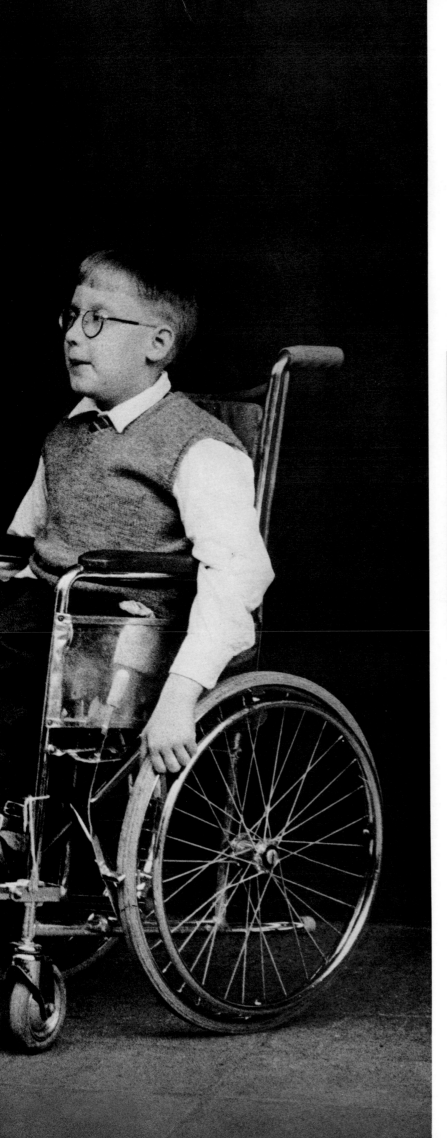

Children afflicted by spina bifida, Coney Hill School in Kent, 1968

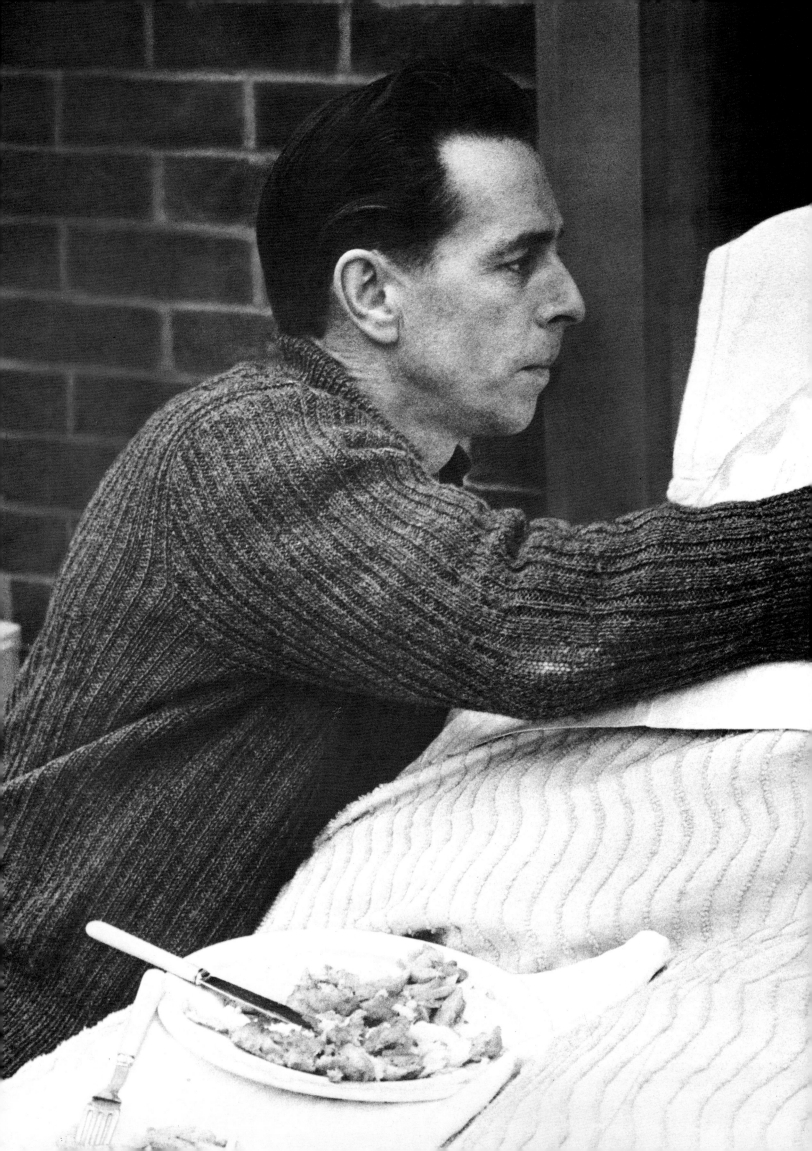

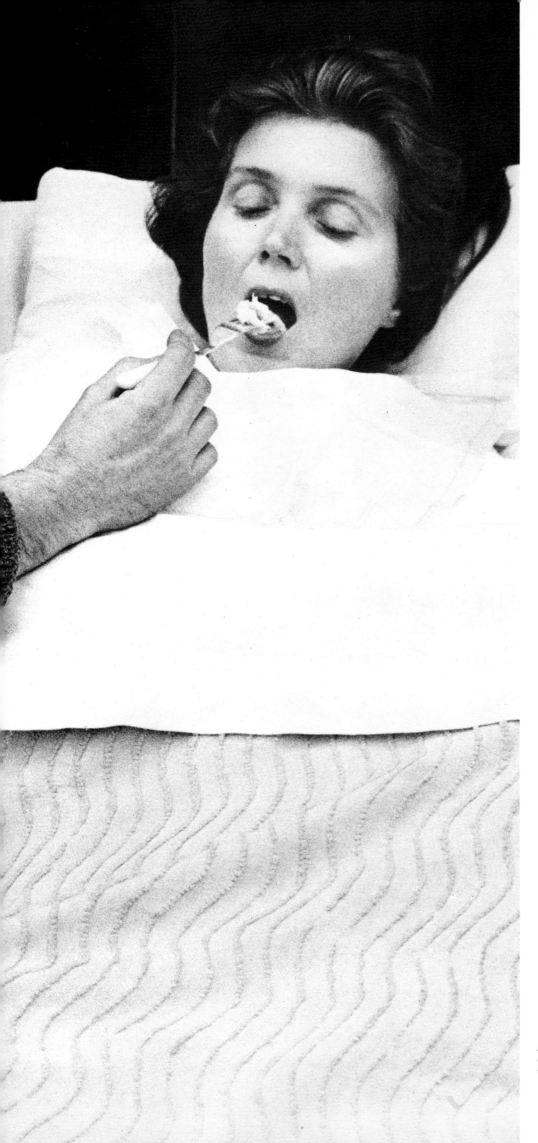

Anne Armstrong, paralysed by polio,
editor of the medical journal 'Responaut',
with her husband, 1965

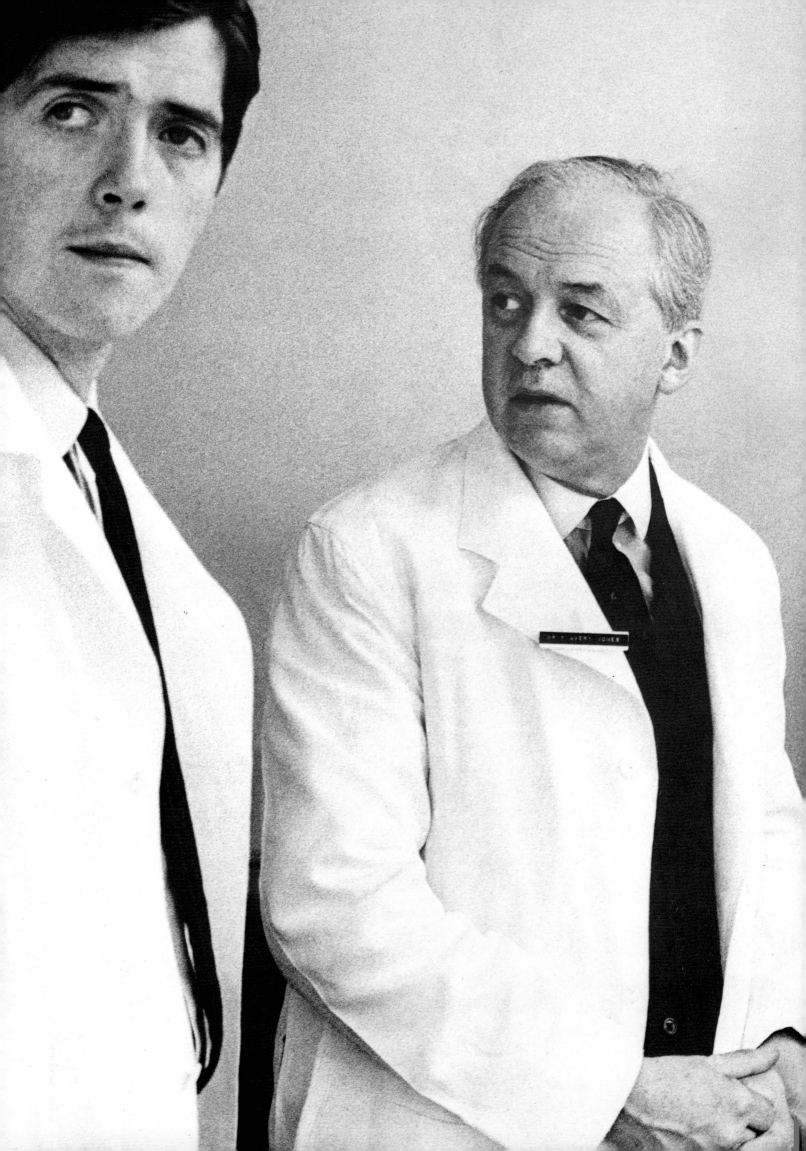

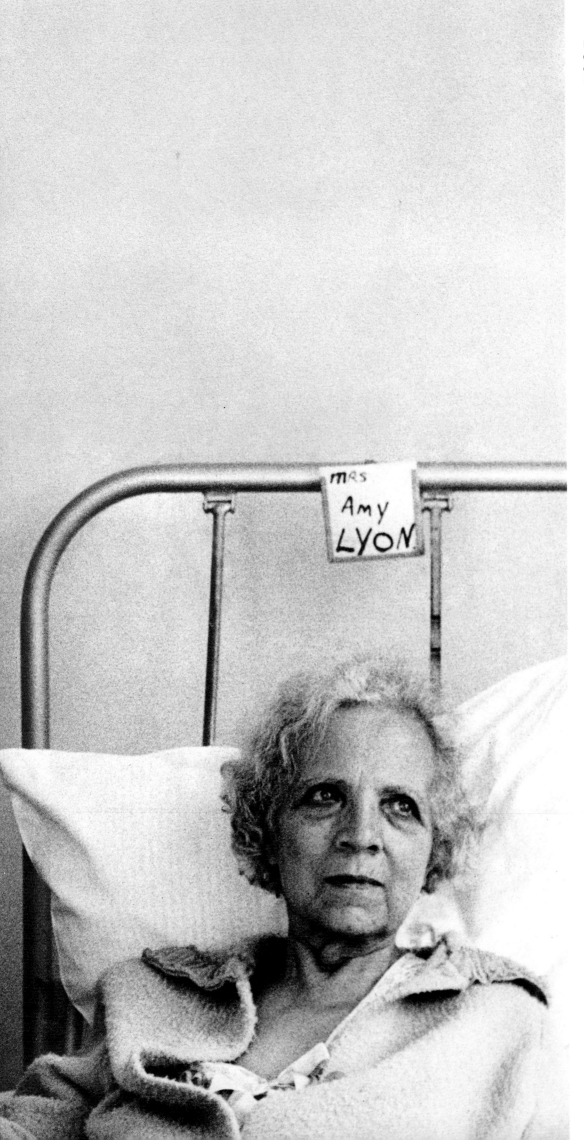

House physician Michael Clarke and
consultant Dr Francis Avery-Jones
on their rounds at London's
Middlesex Hospital, 1967

<u>Overleaf</u> Caring for the mentally ill,
1972 and 1968

151

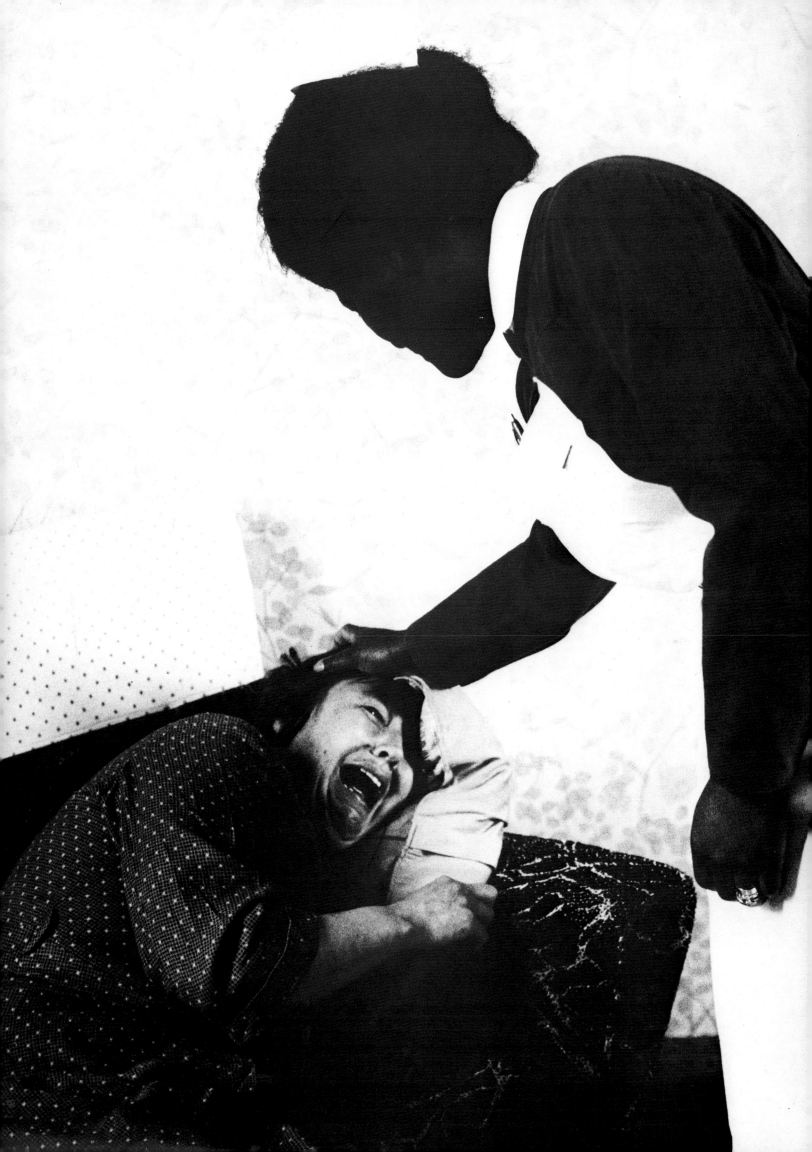

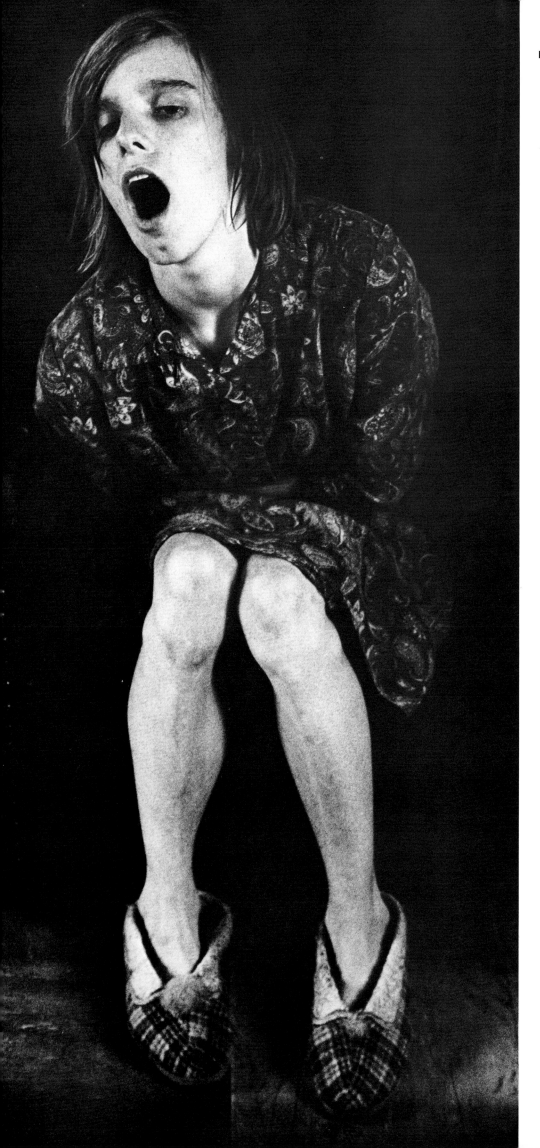

Patients in English mental hospitals, 1968

Overleaf Nursing the mentally ill, 1968

Previous page Mrs Annie Williamson, aged 84, in an old people's home, 1964. Photographing the problems of old age led to the making of the television documentary 'Don't Count the Candles', in 1967

Left A 66-year-old inmate at a mental hospital, his home for the past 43 years, 1968
Below Home for the Incurables, Putney, London, 1976

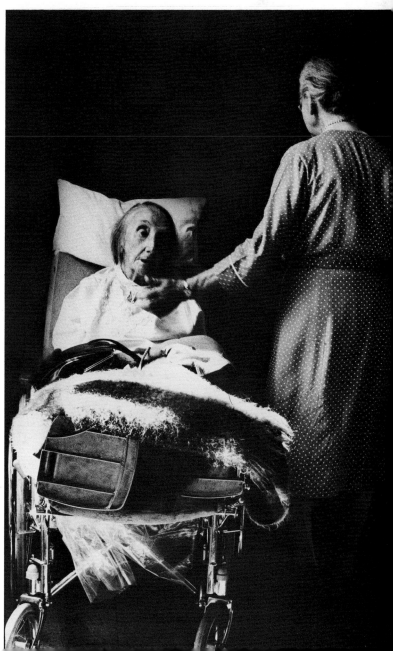

I saw this figure standing on the water's edge at Brighton. We were doing a story on loneliness. Every day, he moved almost imperceptibly in with the tide and out with the tide leaving his shoes at the high water mark. I suddenly realized he was a deaf mute. I talked to him in deaf and dumb language, which I'd learnt at school. He said he lived in a bedsit in Hove and that no one had spoken to him for twenty years.

An old people's home, 1964

Mr Phillips by the Palace Pier, Brighton, 1966

PERFORMERS

I first met Peter Brook when he directed *Ring Round the Moon* and Oliver Messel designed a romantic, baroque greenhouse. As a director, Peter Brook never rants; everything is very quiet; actors are taken off into corners for solo instruction. He is a master of detail; he likes to have full control of everything: the music, the lighting, the props – right through to the taking of stills. In the Fifties he used to come to my studio – which few other old-style directors would think of doing – to discuss the way a photographic session should be tackled. His *Midsummer Night's Dream* (page 168) had the look of a fashion photographer's studio – a white box with lots of reflected light. When I photographed his production of *Antony and Cleopatra* he described the set to me as "*Ring Round the Moon* with straight lines".

**Peter Brook rehearsing his production of
'Antony and Cleopatra' at Stratford-on-Avon, 1978**

Glenda Jackson has a powerful, un-Hollywood face. I always find her convincingly real in any part.
Her unpainted face suits the realism of the modern cinema. She wouldn't have been appreciated in the Thirties.

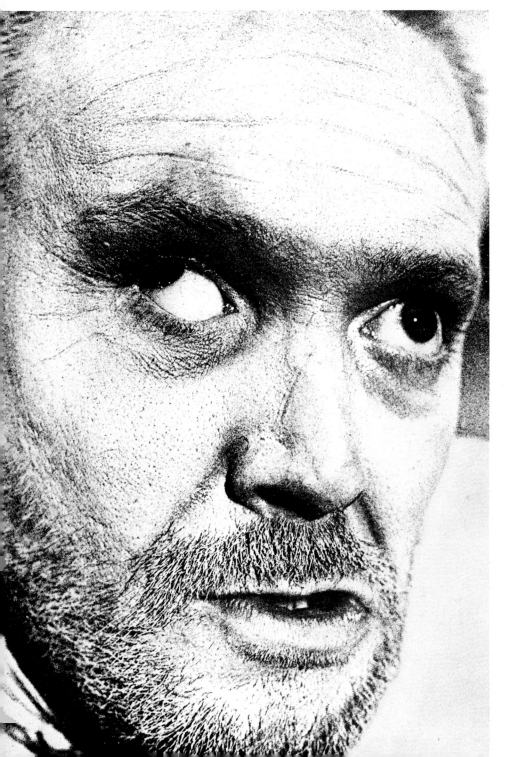

**Right Glenda Jackson as Charlotte Corday in
'Marat-Sade' by Peter Weiss, 1966,
directed by Peter Brook
Left Patrick Magee as the Marquis de Sade
in the same film**

Christopher Gable and Mary
Rutherford as Lysander and Hermia in
'A Midsummer Night's Dream' at
Stratford, directed by Peter Brook, 1970

Photographing Tom Stoppard
just after his success
with *Rosencrantz and
Guildenstern are Dead*,
I found it, as usual, difficult
to know where to start.
I decided to take him down to
a playground in Rotherhithe
which had been made out of
a graveyard, with headstones
round the fence. Perhaps the
thought association was
Hamlet, skull, graveyard.
The first pictures were flat.
Then characteristically he
found the bicycle without
wheels.

Left Tom Stoppard, 1967
**Right Tom Conti, in Brian
Clark's 'Whose Life is it
Anyway?', 1979**

**Overleaf left Maggie Smith and
Robert Stevens in Ingmar
Bergman's production of
'Hedda Gabler', 1970**

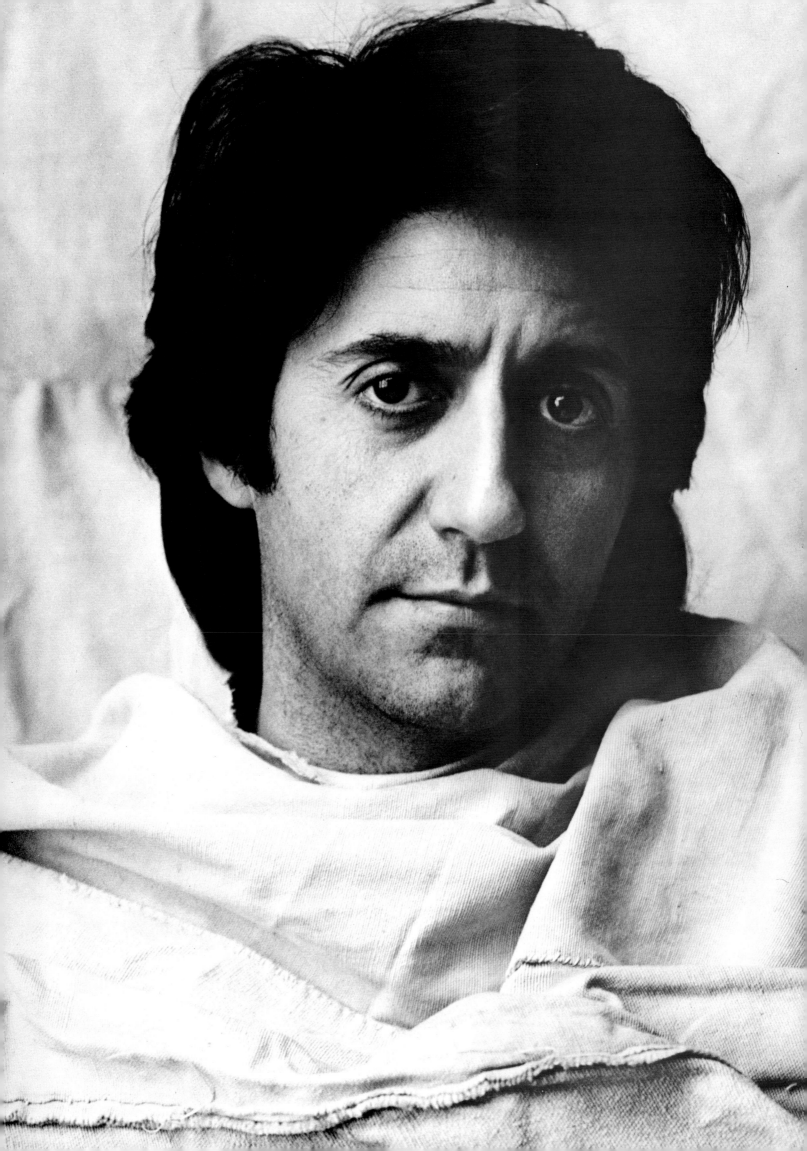

Grace Bumbry was one of the first singers who acted well, bringing realism to her performance. Opera is always difficult to photograph because it is so static: everyone has their mouths open and their eyes shut. I found the ideal place to photograph from is the prompt box. You are close up and sealed off from any distraction. The only hazard is spit.

Grace Bumbry as Amneris in 'Aïda', at Covent Garden, 1968

Inadmissible Evidence is a great play, but very aural. There's very little action and nobody touches anyone. By the time the play was revived at the Royal Court everyone was doing grainy pictures, so I decided to try for a perfectly sharp, clear picture, showing every detail. By chance Nicol Williamson moved his head upwards during one long exposure, which gives the pathos of the character; the rest looked dead in comparison.

On previous page Nicol Williamson as Bill Maitland in 'Inadmissible Evidence' by John Osborne, in 1978. He had played this role in the original production fifteen years previously

To be yourself when being photographed is hard for anyone; it's always easier to hide behind a mask. Comedians stripped of their gags, props, and scripts are nearly always shy, serious and lonely. The Goons (or the Go-on Show as one BBC executive thought it was called) created a totally new sense of British humour through their radio programmes in the Fifties. It's hard to portray the real Spike Milligan and I find it virtually impossible to photograph Sellers as Sellers. Apart from anything else, I know and like him too much. We tend to put off taking photographs and talk endlessly about the latest cameras, electronic gadgets and fast cars. He will go down in history as one of the great performers of our time; and I prefer to be in his company rather than try to capture him realistically on film.

**Two original Goons:
Left Peter Sellers on the
riverbank at Battersea, London,
during the filming of 'The
Optimists of Nine Elms' in 1973
Right Spike Milligan, 1957**

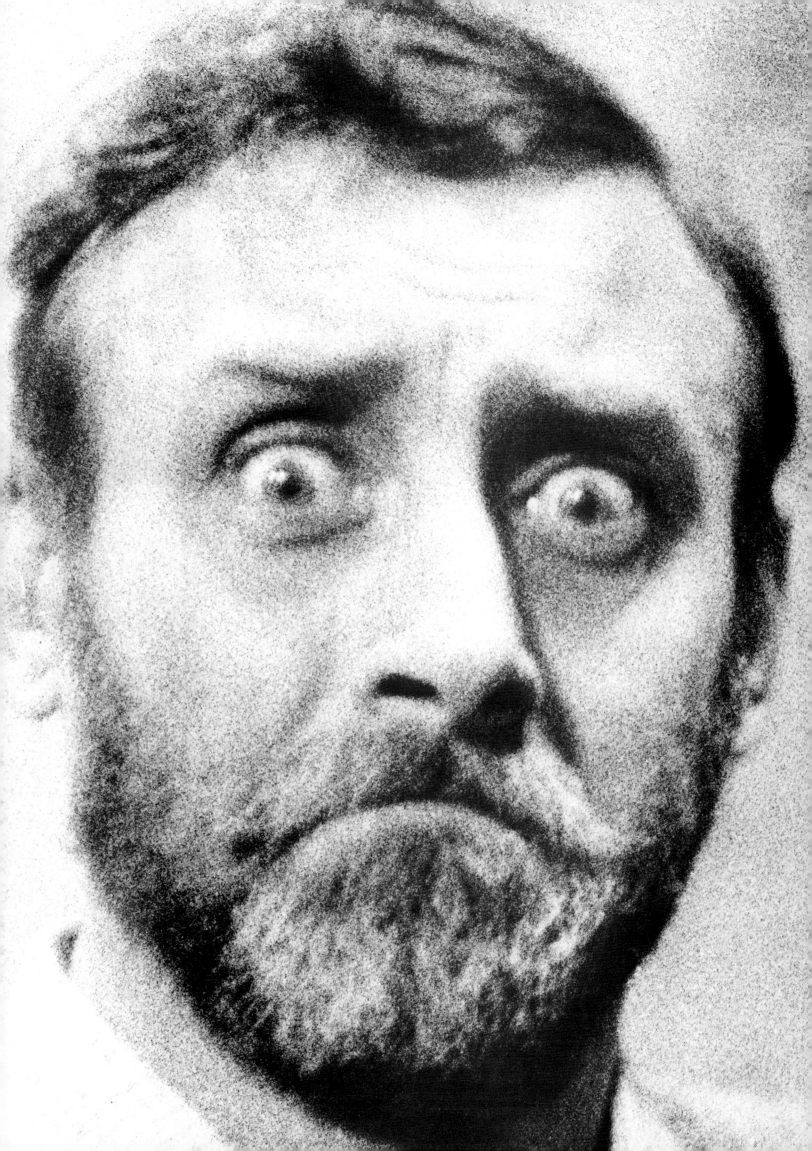

At lunch Chaplin said would we like to see one of his films, and of course we were thrilled at the privilege of being able to watch one of his legendary classics with the master himself. We sat back, expecting to see *Modern Times* with Chaplin actually working the projector. It turned out to be a home movie of him and Oona on a wild life trip to Uganda six months before. It was rather jerky.

Charlie Chaplin, Vevey, Switzerland, 1964

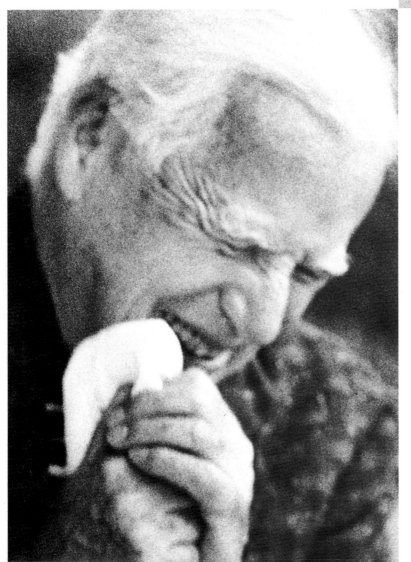

In Italy the paparazzi, sneaky long-lens photographers riding motor-scooters, are a plague. When we went there to photograph Sophia Loren, I asked my assistant to keep his eyes open and warn me if he saw anyone. The Villa Ponti, outside Rome, however, was well guarded, with high walls and tight security. We had to ring three times at the gate to get in. My assistant thought I was making a fuss about nothing. I spent two days photographing Loren and Ponti and took pictures of Loren in the grounds of the Villa. Two weeks after the sitting, a magazine published a double-page spread of me taking pictures of her. What I liked most was that my outside pictures were under-exposed, whereas those taken by the paparazzi from the bushes had come out beautifully.

<u>Overleaf</u> **Sophia Loren and Carlo Ponti, 1970**

I 'knew' Bette Davis so well through the cinema, from such an early age, that I found it unnerving to meet her for the first time on location. I wasn't allowed to take stills of her until she was ready. It was two days before she gave me a look that said Yes. She didn't think very much of having to make a film in the sticky heat of Egypt and couldn't understand why they hadn't just built the set somewhere outside Los Angeles.

I needed to photograph Mia Farrow in the part of Daisy in *The Great Gatsby* before there were any costumes. I went with Barney Wan, *Vogue*'s Design Consultant, to the Kensington Antiques Market, and he picked out some clothes. We took Miss Farrow to Chiswick House. It was between Christmas and New Year, early morning and bitterly cold. We gave her an old string vest with the shoulder straps cut off, to wear as a tube under the chiffon dress. As we were only taking head and shoulders shots she was able to wear gumboots and have a paraffin stove between her legs.

Bette Davis in 'Death on the Nile', 1977

Mia Farrow in 'The Great Gatsby', 1972

Taking stills on a film set is frustrating. You can only work between takes, and then in silence. The camera and crew are, of course, in the best position and you are stuck with their over-powerful lighting, and from the side the set doesn't work: you see the mechanics of make-believe, and beyond the stars their stand-ins knitting and drinking cups of tea. With both the Agatha Christie films I took the actors away from the set and made portraits of them in the mood of the characters they were playing. I gave them one prop each. Photographing them against plain backgrounds, I wanted them to look like 'Spy' caricatures.

With *Death on the Nile* on location in Egypt I bought a felucca sail and made it into a tent, influenced by the plain set Irving Penn used for his classic photographs of tradesmen. I was able to take the tent wherever the film crew went. It was practical because I could get the actors away in quiet moments when they weren't needed on the set. I brought the felucca sail home and still use it, for example to wrap round Tom Conti (page 171) to recreate the feeling of his bedridden performance in *Whose Life is it Anyway?*

Two Inspector Poirots:
Albert Finney, left, in 'Murder on the Orient Express',
1974 and Peter Ustinov, right, in 'Death on the Nile', 1977

DRESS DESIGNERS

Costume designer Anthony Powell,
who won his second Oscar for 'Death on the Nile', 1976

In the Fifties Audrey Withers, the editor of *Vogue*, sent me to photograph Dior. She gave me detailed instructions. "I want a picture that will capture his whole glittering empire, *everything* he has done and designed for women in the world," she said. I imagined having to do a great montage of stockings and scent and clothes, but she continued, "I want you to go to his home in the South of France and," she paused, "I think the only thing that will sum up *all* his achievement . . . is to photograph him in close-up against a perfectly plain white background."

Much later, in the Seventies, I was asked by French *Vogue* to go to Paris and photograph all the major designers. They had an actress, Dayle Haddon, who was to model each designer's clothes. I had no idea how to do it, and there was hardly any time – I was expected to photograph three or four of them a day. So I decided to go back to what I used to do with the English *Vogue* fashion shots in the Fifties, to tell a continuing story. My idea was to have Dayle as a girl that all designers happened to be in love with. Each designer would be entertaining her in his own mood.

It all went wrong to start with. I was using a big camera and lights, and the atmosphere was too formal. I reverted to a smaller camera, and no lights, and made the whole thing much more informal. Some of the designers were very stiff and dignified. Gérard Pipart of Nina Ricci, in the picnic scene, wouldn't relax easily, so I got Dayle to tickle him without warning. Angelo Tarlazzi of Patou entered much more into the spirit of things for a picture in his bathroom. He didn't know Dayle was going to turn on the shower, but when she did he retaliated, and the sitting broke up into chaos.

There were setbacks. With Courrèges we were going to shoot in his fashion house. We were too late; they were giving us lunch – perhaps they'd left the stove on – anyway, the house caught fire and when we arrived there were fire engines lining the street. The place was gutted. I thought we might shoot in the charred remains, but Courrèges was too upset. We changed locations.

Christian Dior, 1957

Dayle Haddon in Paris with Madame Grès, 1976

. . . with Jules-François Crahay of Lanvin on the Champs Elysées

. . . with Gérard Pipart of Nina Ricci

DRESSING UP

Barbara Cartland, 1976

Barbara Cartland is unique. When I arrived with a Leica and a reflector board, I soon realized she was unimpressed by my lack of equipment and small camera; she is more accustomed to spotlights than daylight. But thoughtfully she keeps a store of her own lights and gives detailed instructions where to put them. She is very kind. She offers visiting cameramen rejuvenating pills as well as lights. The pills made me rather sleepy. She has a labrador she likes and a prettier dog she is photographed with. Having seen many similar shots of Miss Cartland, I decided to take her out into the snow – it's about the biggest reflector board I could find; but this photograph, with her favourite lighting, is the one she liked.

Danny La Rue, 1970

Left Ginger Rogers in
New York, 1968

Right William Douglas Home,
playwright, at his home in
Hampshire, 1977

Above Sir Robert Helpmann and
below Sir Frederick Ashton, as the
Ugly Sisters in 'Cinderella'
at Covent Garden, 1965

David Bowie, 1978

Rudolf Nureyev in Ken Russell's 'Valentino', 1977

Rodney Marsh, Queen's Park Rangers soccer star, 1972

Tsuyoshi Kshiwada, Sumo wrestler, Japan, 1967

BALLET

Ballet has always been part of my life since I was introduced to it early on by my uncle, Oliver Messel. The music, I'm afraid, means little to me beyond its rhythm; I'm tone deaf. I admire the shapes, I just watch the physical movement – how well someone can move, leap or turn.

I learnt about ballet photography from Baron. He was the leading ballet photographer of his day. Like McBean in the theatre, he would set up the whole thing artificially on the stage, but he did at least take action pictures. He used an electronic flash-gun, which was very new in those days.

I find ballet photography fairly unsatisfactory. For theatre photography you can use the medium of the camera to get closer to the mood of the play. With ballet you go down a step. Classical ballet is designed to be seen only from the front. On stage there's so much light on the dancers, especially if they're in white, that the exposure is way out for anything in the background, so that it goes black, which is boring. The human eye is so much more sensitive than film. If you are bored by the dancer your eye can admire the set. All the photographer can do is record from the best angle.

I don't believe in the motorized camera which everyone uses today. Although you can take a

**Left Dame Marie Rambert, 88, taking
class at the Ballet Rambert School in Chiswick, London, 1976
Above Dame Ninette de Valois, and pupil, 1974**

picture at every fifth of a second it can still miss *the* moment when the hand or leg is perfectly stretched. You should be able to rely on your own reflex action and capture it in a single shot.

I find it much more interesting to take another kind of picture, in the freedom of a ballet school or during rehearsals, with the reality of a dancer's ordinary rehearsal clothes and using daylight. Then I can see the relationship between the dancer and the choreographer, as they work something out together. If two dancers show a sympathy, as Rudolf Nureyev and Margot Fonteyn did, then it is much better to catch that feeling when it emerges for the first time, in rehearsal, rather than when you see it repeated for the umpteenth time at Covent Garden.

Ballet photography depends largely upon fast reactions, to freeze a dancer in space or capture a perfect lift. Exactly like the Muybridge photographs taken in the 1870s which showed for the first time the sequence of a horse's legs galloping, the ballet photograph can freeze a moment the eye never sees.

Left **Prima Ballerina Tamara Karsavina, who danced with Nijinsky, aged 73, 1958**
Right **Dame Margot Fonteyn and Rudolf Nureyev rehearsing together for 'Marguérite and Armand', 1963. This ballet was written especially for them by Frederick Ashton**

Nureyev's move to the West was an injection of adrenalin to ballet. Not only is he technically superb, but he is also a charismatic star. Every moment he is on stage, whether he is dancing or motionless, every eye in the theatre, male and female, whether they admit it or not, is watching only him. When ballet was considered an art only for the elite, *Life* commissioned me to photograph his *Swan Lake* in Vienna and published eleven pages, which was unheard of for a ballet story.

Baryshnikov on stage is an extraordinary combination of weightlessness and precision: off stage he is unassuming and untemperamental. Now he is the hottest name in New York, but when I first photographed him for *Vogue* in 1972, before he moved to the West, he was unknown: my assistant filed him as 'Russian Dancer'.

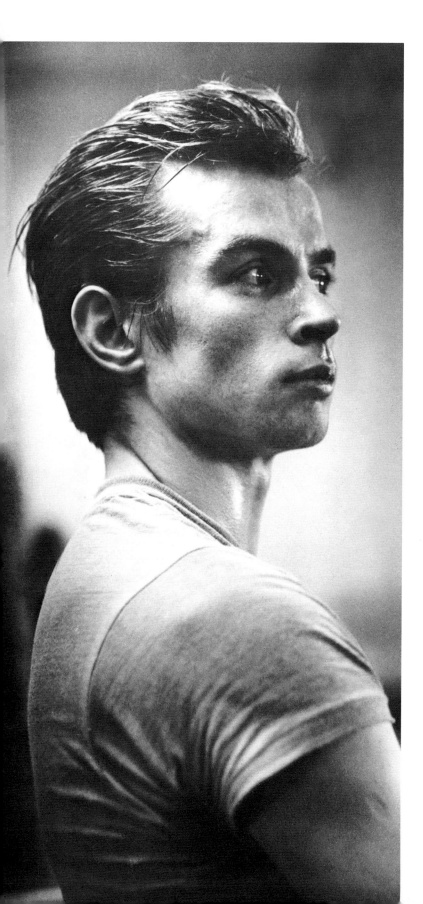

Left Rudolf Nureyev in rehearsal for 'Giselle', 1962
Right Mikhail Baryshnikov, 1977. In his first three years' work with the American Ballet Company he danced thirty different roles

Overleaf Baryshnikov, 1977 and 1972
Pages 210–11: Members of the Netherlands Dance Theatre in 'Mutations', 1971

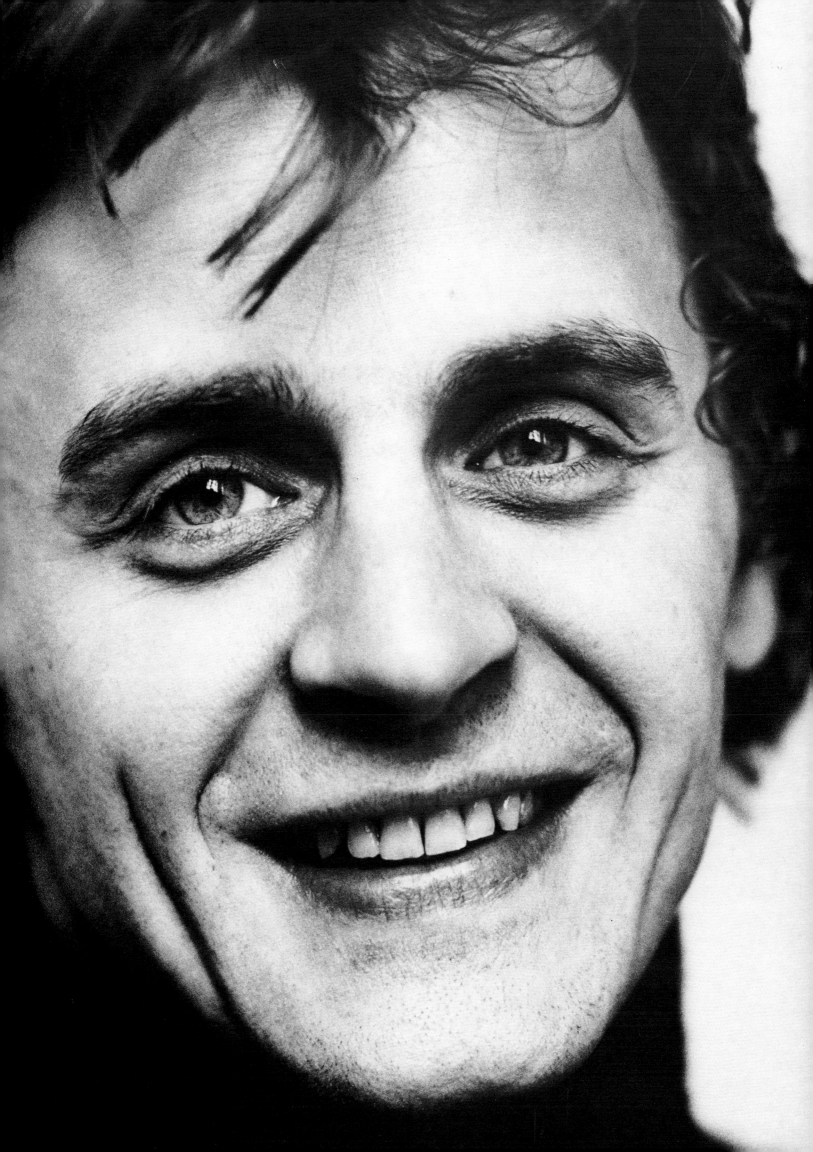

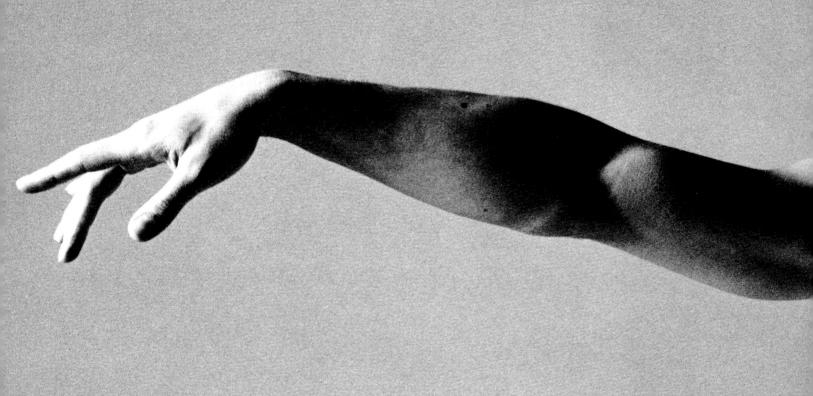

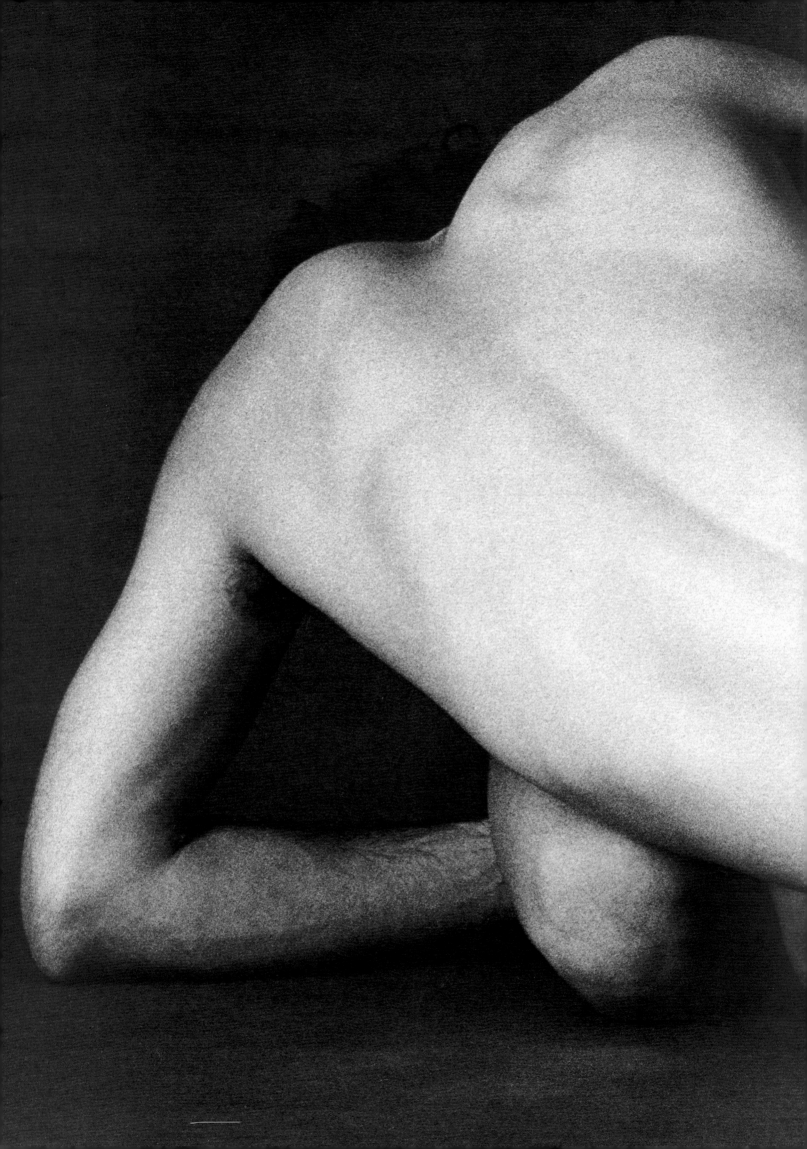

Arthur Mitchell started the Dance Theater of Harlem in the basement of a disused church, and in the process created much more than a ballet school. Having made his name as a dancer, unlike most people who come out of Harlem and make a success, he went back there. He rescued teenagers off the streets and gave them a chance to do something worthwhile – from painting sets to making scenery and dancing. At first some of the boys thought dancing was cissy. So Arthur would ask them if they had a girlfriend and suggested they bring them the next day. And then he'd say, "OK, you're so tough, lift her up with one hand above your head." And of course they couldn't. He showed them dance was something to do with athletics, physique and their own culture.

No one wanted to publish my pictures. The editor of one American magazine said, "We've filled up our quota of features on blacks for this year." A great choreographer and teacher, Arthur Mitchell gave Harlem the kind of culture the rest of New York takes for granted.

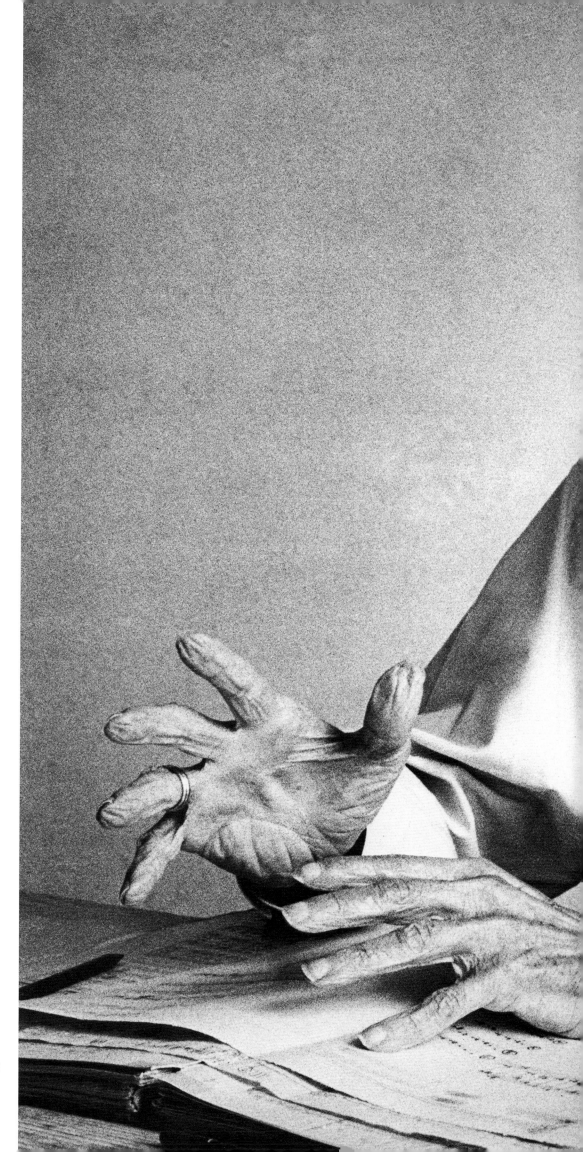

Igor Stravinsky, aged 89, 1971

ESCAPISM

I like colour that is impressionistic and mysterious rather than real. Accurate and pedantic colour seems to me only suitable for advertising, for frost on bottles or for the bloom on grapes. I admire the swirling, blurred action pictures of Ernst Haas and the soft, grainy colour of Sarah Moon. Pure reality recorded in colour seems to me to be like a data book – true, but uninspiring.

Misusing film can help you to get away from clichés. The advice on film packs makes for boring pictures; reading the instruction 'backwards' makes for freshness. The 'don'ts' can get more interesting results than the 'do's'. I like to push film so the grain works for me. Cheap copying processes can also transform transparencies into something new. Technical mistakes in colour often make for better pictures – by leaving out one colour plate in the printing or by over-exposing. The white horse overleaf was photographed in a paddock surrounded by smoke bombs which killed the background (and kept the horses on the move), and over-exposure stopped it looking like a post-card. It's lack of colour I like best. In fact I don't see in colour, I see shapes. The examples of colour forced on the public by film manufacturers are always too bright, too brash and sharp for my liking. I like to catch subtle images that can linger in people's minds.

Above **John Aspinall, gambler and zoo owner, 1973**

Rodeo, Texas, 1974

Pages 218–23 Shire horse and blacksmith at Whitbread's London Brewery, 1978;
Emaus, Arab stallion in Maryland, 1967; Goliath Heron in Uganda, 1964; White Beluga whales, 1968

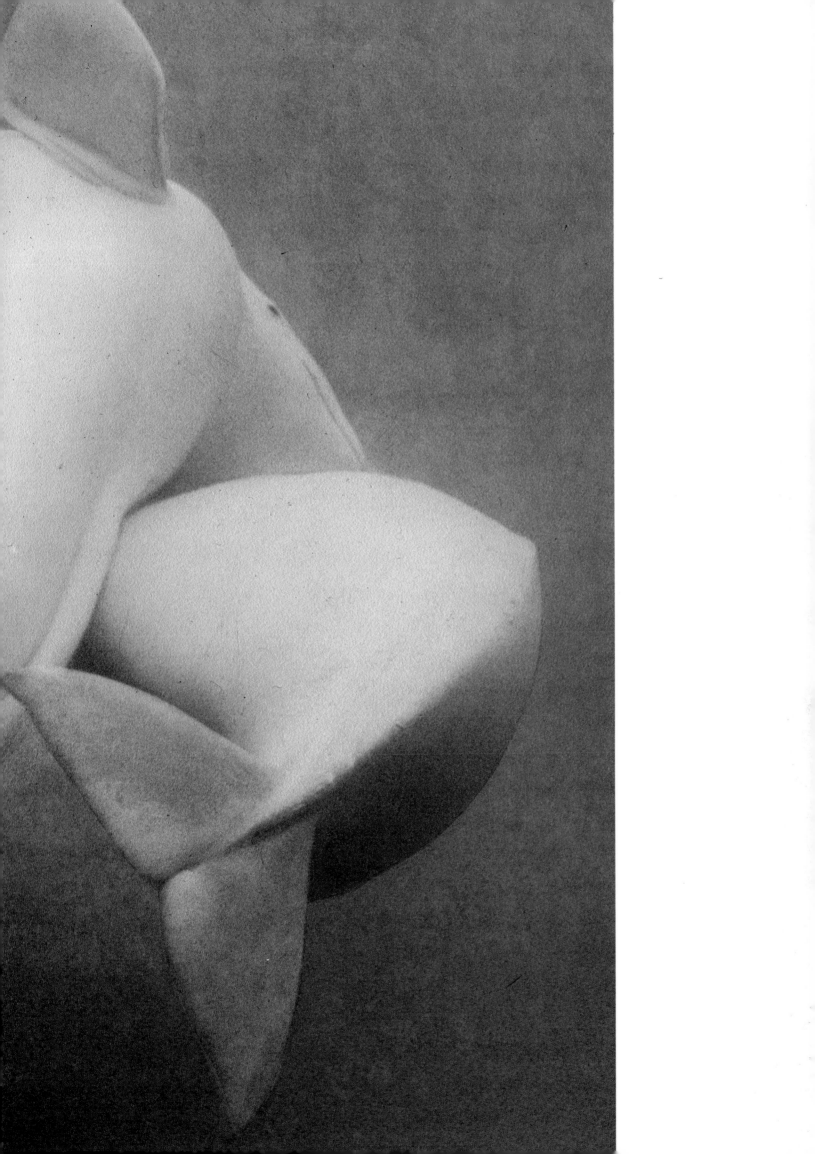

GENERATIONS

Mother and child, Cusco, Peru, 1972

Left **Rabbits used for laboratory tests, Bangkok, 1976**

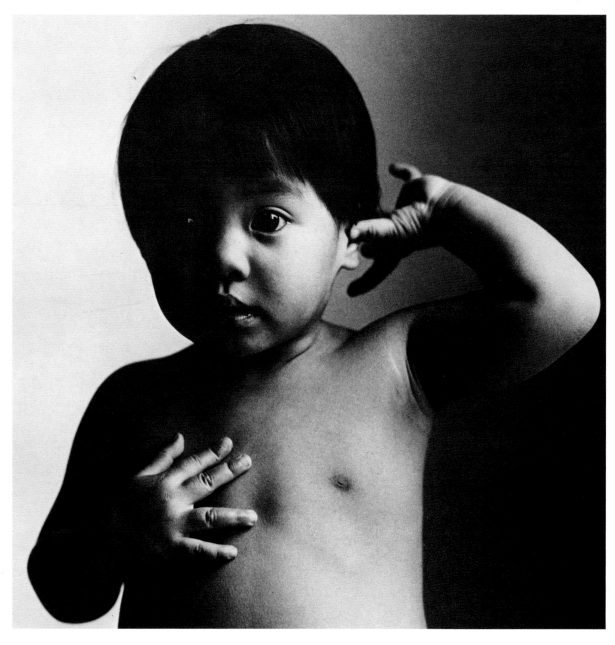

Abigail Ackroyd, aged 17 months, formerly Pham Thanh Mai of Saigon, 1969

Claire Hood, aged 7, in the musical 'Annie', London, 1978

Princess Anne, 1969

Dame Edith Evans, 1977

Dame Sybil Thorndike, 1956

Evgenia Citkovitz, aged 16, 1979

Lady Diana Cooper, aged 84, 1977

Princess Alice, Countess of Athlone,
aged 95, with a photograph of
her grandmother, Queen Victoria, 1978

Her Majesty the Queen with her first grandson Peter,
the great, great, great, great grandson of Queen Victoria, 1978

STAND-INS

David Linley, assistant, as Princess Alice, 1978

Ondine, 1970

Anthony Dowell, August 3rd 1976

Yves St Laurent, August 2nd 1976

Photographing people varies totally: one day I'm alone with a miniature camera trying to capture a moment that is typical; the next can be an enormous production with hairdressers equipped with tongs, lacquer and wigs, make-up artists standing by ready to camouflage any small defect or repaint an entire face, fashion editors poised with accessories ranging from bracelets to bulldog clips and assistants balancing reflector boards and white umbrellas to control the light.

The session often starts at dawn and lasts for twelve hours; most of the time is spent in set building and endless titivation, moving furniture if indoors, or transforming the landscape if outside – anything from putting a matchbox behind a looking glass so as not to catch my own reflection to planting shrubs to hide a pylon. It's utter make-believe and romantic fantasy achieved by downright, but harmless, cheating; it is about as far away from my documentary work as I can get.

I need an immediate playback to see whether I'm getting the right effect so I use a polaroid attachment on the back of my camera to check the composition, special effects and depth of field. Rather than exhaust, bore, freeze or broil the main character, I use stand-ins – assistants, editors, hairdressers, make-up artists. I always keep the polaroids as they are amusing to look back on, like a scrapbook or photographic diary, reminding me of the lengths we went to to achieve a seemingly simple result.

Ondine romantically emerging from a misty lake was in fact taken on a November morning. The model, wearing an army string vest under her costume and gum boots, stood in a submerged thermos filled with hot water; the mist was smouldering leaves soaked in paraffin. Before photographing Anthony Dowell as Romeo, I took a preliminary polaroid. An ashen white and shaking assistant, whom I hadn't worked with before, handed me the result. There, inexplicably, to him, was Dowell surrounded by a flock of non-existent sheep. I had been photographing Yves St Laurent the day before in his Paris garden sitting with his plastic sheep, but had forgotten to pull out the last polaroid.

Felicity Clark, beauty editor, as Princess Anne

Princess Anne and her son, Peter, 1978

Anthony Clavet, make-up artist, as Flora Fraser

Flora Fraser, 1979

Princess Michael of Kent, 3 July 1979, 9 a.m.

Princess Michael and son, 4 p.m.

INDEX